CONTEMPORARY CLASSICS

CONTEMPORARY CLASSICS
FURNITURE OF THE MASTERS

Charles D. Gandy, FASID, *and Susan Zimmermann-Stidham*

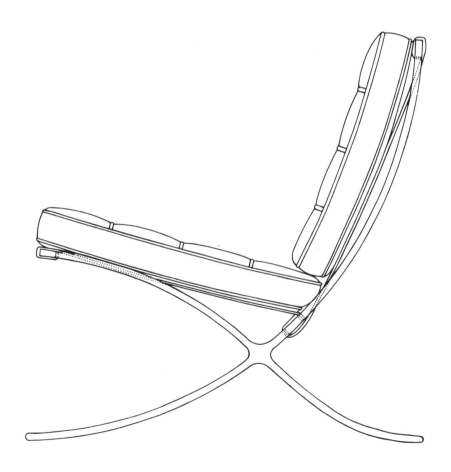

WHITNEY LIBRARY OF DESIGN
An imprint of Watson-Guptill Publications
New York

Book designed by Naomi Auerbach, in collaboration with the authors.

Copyright 1981 © by Charles D. Gandy and Susan Zimmermann-Stidham

Originally published by McGraw-Hill, Inc. in 1981 under the same title.

This edition first published in 1990 by Whitney Library of Design,
an imprint of Watson-Guptill Publications,
a division of BPI Communications, Inc.,
1515 Broadway, New York, N.Y. 10036

Library of Congress Cataloging-in-Publication Data

Gandy, Charles D.
    Contemporary classics: furniture of the masters/Charles D.
Gandy, Susan Zimmermann-Stidham.
      p. cm.
    Reprint. Originally published: New York: McGraw-Hill, c1981.
    Includes bibliographical references and index.
    ISBN 0-8230-0931-9
    1. Furniture—History—20th century. 2. Decoration and ornament—
International style.   I. Zimmermann-Stidham, Susan.   II. Title.
NK2397.G36   1990
749.2'049—dc20   90-39588
                                             CIP

Distributed in the United Kingdom by Phaidon Press Ltd.,
Musterlin House, Jordan Hill Road, Oxford OX2 8DP

Printed in U.S.A.

First printing, 1990

1 2 3 4 5 6 7 8/96 95 94 93 92 91 90

To our friends . . . where would we be without them?

Contents

Preface

In our professional experience, it has become clear that few concise references dealing with the major designs of Contemporary furniture exist. The present volume evolved from a need expressed increasingly by professionals, educators, students, and the design-conscious public. The text does not attempt to cover the field of Contemporary furniture design completely; rather, it provides a focused introduction to the subject matter. Short historical essays are followed by biographical synopses of the designers, accurately scaled drawings of their "classic" designs, and pertinent historical information concerning the development of each piece discussed. An illustrator's sketch of each designer and a reproduction of his signature add a personal touch. This format, we believe, lends itself to the emergence of a concept of "classic" furniture, particular to the present time.

In the early stages of research, we had to determine our selective criteria. What definitional boundaries allow us to call a particular design a "Contemporary classic"? First, it is necessary to define a "classic." Briefly, a classic possesses quality, adheres to an established set of artistic standards, and consequently becomes an influential model for subsequent designs.

Quality, a concrete characteristic, connotes excellence in materials and methods of construction. A Louis XVI bureau by David Roentgen or a Barcelona chair by Ludwig Mies van der Rohe offers sufficient illustration of this timeless factor. But quality alone is not enough to distinguish a classic; also necessary is an awareness of the abstract element of aesthetics. Having been interpreted by changing societies, the basic elements and principles of design such as scale, rhythm, and proportion have had changing roles in the development of this awareness. However perceived, they have governed the realm of creativity and imagination throughout the centuries. Working together, the two principles of quality and aesthetics are the forces behind the continual copying and recopying of a design.

A Contemporary classic differs from a traditional one insofar as these principles of quality and aesthetics adapt to the needs of each age. Since the early nineteenth century, machine production has gradually replaced handcraftsmanship, and a new theory of furniture design has evolved. New construction techniques, new materials, and a changing attitude toward design have produced a more functional type of furniture that is accessible and adaptable to our rapid-paced, fluctuating environment. A lack of surface decoration characterizes the resulting style; beauty becomes dependent on form and honesty of materials and construction. Thus, appropriateness to the industrialized age distinguishes a Contemporary classic from a traditional classic.

We have strived for simplicity and accuracy in presenting both the written text and the drawings. Authentication of many of our findings was possible because Europe, the birthplace of the Contemporary movement, was our base of study. We verified information found contradictory in other sources. For example, who first applied the cantilever principle in furniture construction: Stam, Mies, or Breuer? Was Hans J. Wegner a student of the influential teacher and furniture designer Klaare Klint? Whenever possible personal interviews took place with each designer, a representative of the designer, or an associate. Consequently, we gained firsthand insights into the development of many designs.

Simplicity and accuracy are also reflected in the scaled furniture drawings, which are based on information obtained from the offices of the designers or the current manufacturers. Too frequently, drawings tend to be either overly technical, losing the attention of the layman, or too spare in detail, arousing criticism from professional circles. Our drawings strike a mean: They are simple in their presentation, yet accurate in their detail.

All of the works featured in this book meet our criteria for selection and presentation. Only the most influential designers and their most outstanding work are included: pieces of furniture truly deserving the distinction of being known as Contemporary classics.

Charles D. Gandy
Atlanta, Georgia

Susan Zimmermann-Stidham
Lucerne, Switzerland

Acknowledgments

Special thanks to:
  Elissa Aalto
  Marcel Breuer
  Hans J. Wegner
  Ray Eames

and to:

Bob Allen, The New South Drawing Co., Atlanta, Georgia; The American College in Lucerne, Switzerland; Atelier International, Ltd., New York; Herbert Beckard, Marcel Breuer and Associates, New York; Mary Frances Carter, Auburn University, Auburn, Alabama; Anna Casati, Cassina S.p.A., Milan, Italy; Frances Drew, Georgia Institute of Technology, Atlanta, Georgia; Svend Dubdahl, CH/RY/SW ApS, Vejen, Denmark; Ludwig Glaeser, Mies van der Rohe Archives, The Museum of Modern Art, New York; James Grady, Georgia Institute of Technology, Atlanta, Georgia; Poul Hansen, Johannes Hannsen AS, Copenhagen, Denmark; Pat Hoffman, International Contract Furnishings, New York; Cheryl Howard, Atlanta, Georgia; Jørgen and Esther Jensen, House of Denmark, Atlanta, Georgia; Yvonne Kozlowski, Auburn University, Auburn, Alabama; Georg Thonet, Gebrüder Thonet, Frankenberg, Germany; Ake T. Tjeder, Artek, OY AB, Helsinki, Finland; Phillis McCullough, Thonet, York, Pennsylvania; Bill McGehee, Knoll International, Inc., Atlanta, Georgia; Goran Schildt, Tammisaari, Finland; Donald Rorke, Knoll International, Inc., New York; Karin Schulz, Herman Miller, AG, Basel, Switzerland;

and very special thanks to:

Agnes McLendon, for her captivating illustrations; Ralph W. Miller, Jr., for his unending diligence in editing and redacting; Keri Z. Allen, for her meticulous line drawings; and Bruno Zimmermann, for his continued patience and understanding.

Introduction

Contemporary society is quite different from that of previous epochs—a fact of foremost importance to the creators of furniture. Traditional furniture makers catered to the financially elite classes. Design richness was equated with affluence. Quality was a constant, controlled by highly trained designers and craftsmen. But the events of the nineteenth century altered this situation.

The industrialization of handcrafts made cheap imitations of antiques available to an expanding middle class whose taste revealed that quality was not a prerequisite in the selection of their furnishings. Design reformers of the mid-century criticized the degeneracy of these mass-produced products and the decorators who created them. Progressive designers returned to the traditional values of quality and beauty in an effort to provide more appropriate furnishings for the new, more pluralistic society.

Twentieth-century designers have faced the same challenge. Modern clientele also vary in cultural background, pocketbook, and the role they place on furniture. An array of designs has resulted, varying in appearance and technique not only from decade to decade, but also within the portfolios of individual designers. When surveying the furniture of today's market, one cannot help wondering what creative process gave birth to the dissociated menagerie which is collectively referred to as Contemporary furniture. To be sure, common convictions exist, and hereditary traits can be discerned. A deeper look at the historical background will shed light on the evolution of twentieth-century designer furniture.

In the decorative eras preceding the Industrial Revolution, the master craftsman, the *maître-ébéniste,* supplied a discriminating clientele a quality of craftsmanship and materials that only they could afford. Both designer and patron valued the latest innovations in materials and technology as well as current fashions.

For the most part international trends originating in Europe's ruling courts dictated the styling of this handcrafted furniture. As design movements spread across Europe and America, a national flavoring was usually added. This domestic styling as well as the international movements themselves in general drew inspiration from a variety of sources: the private whims of monarchs; archeological rediscoveries of ancient civilizations; or contact with new cultures either through war or through trade.

To the delight of students of traditional furniture history, motifs or key decorative features characterize the bulk of design in each trend. Traits such as general character of line, technique of carving, style of leg, and newly introduced ornamentation served as unifying devices and labels of identification, but they also had more subtle roles to play. As a luxury feature, they affirmed the social status of the owner. In France, the incorporation of peasant motifs during the reign of Louis XVI provided the ruling class with a fanciful distraction from the nation's political problems. Motifs also frequently expressed awe or kinship with previous empires, as, for example, in Napoleon's revival of Roman ornament in the early nineteenth century. Aside from their source or purpose, the decorative movements inspired harmony and consistency in traditional interiors. In the hands of the cabinetmaker, decorative purity as well as superlative materials and techniques were assured.

The nineteenth century witnessed the birth of a new epoch in which machine work replaced handwork. Unfortunately, the changeover succeeded in astonishing its contemporaries instead of inspiring them. Spreading through North Atlantic countries, the Industrial Revolution redistributed wealth and restructured the classes of traditional society. It made quite an impression on the business of furniture design as well. The fashion-conscious nouveau riche craved lavish decoration as an assertion of their new social standing. Victorian designers of mass-produced furniture contented themselves and public tastes by copying past decorative styles—no matter how ill-suited the result to its age. Under these conditions the once prestigious furniture guilds and the quality and esteem of design that they had assured disappeared. To compete with the machine was vain: it could furnish new residences with "stylish" possessions for a fraction of the cost of the original handcrafted goods.

The Victorian home was a private fortress of protection from the confusion of the outside world. Heavy, dark interiors provided a setting in which to display the clutter of one's newly acquired belongings. The growing market of eager consumers had a fanatic interest in historic styling that blended with Victorian inventiveness and technology to create some of the most hideous contraptions and objets d'art found in civilized times. The furniture industries of England and continental Europe dabbled in every major traditional style; Empire, Biedermeier, Louis XV, Gothic, and Oriental all cascaded onto the consumer market. Americans followed, with added emphasis placed on mechanical gadgetry. Quality traditional materials and methods were simulated, and traditional forms bastardized. Frequently conflicting styles were combined in one piece, with motifs thoughtlessly applied. With each item fighting for emphasis, the various styles converged in the drawing and music rooms of the new connoisseurs. The ostentatious hideaway was complete.

A drastic change was needed. Though industrialization had been the major impetus for this design upset, technology was not solely responsible. The dynamic new vocabulary of materials and construction techniques only provided a means for mass-producing products veneered in the stale grandeur of the past, but it could have challenged the imagination of the design world. When handled correctly, new materials—such as plywood, steel, and glass—and new techniques—such as metal plating and the bending and molding of wood—would become building blocks of a new design movement aiming to replace the popular Victorian furniture.

Once the positive aspects of industry were recognized in the early 1900s, all that remained unsettled was the question of styling. Historical decoration with its frivolous surface enrichment was out. The vulgarity of Victorian misuse only hastened the conclusion of early twentieth-century designers that ornament simply was not needed as a source of beautification on modern furniture any more than on the modern airplane, automobile, or telephone. The practicality of these utilitarian forms, as well as their materials and production, gradually began to attract the attention of pre-World War I designers. Amidst the tempo and diversity of modern life-styles, the functional approach to design was finally recognized as the key to a Contemporary aesthetic.

In this environment the first successful design solutions of the twentieth century were presented during the 1920s. Public attitudes toward furniture had changed. Designers had finally developed a sensitivity to production, material, and function. But it had taken over seventy years to progress from the early pleas for reform to this Contemporary mind set.

The Arts and Crafts Movement: A Philosophical Beginning

Contemporary furniture was first conceived as playing a vital role in social reform—an awkward function which survived well into the twentieth century. The philosophical lineage of this idea can be traced to mid-nineteenth-century England, the birthplace of the Industrial Revolution. In spite of the advantages of technological progress there was an acute awareness of its negative social repercussions.

William Morris (1834–1896) was the first of a long line of renowned furniture designers convinced of the moral need for better furnishings. But he was not the first to condemn Victorian industrialized products. Preceding him, Henry Cole (1808–1882) had encouraged better-quality construction as early as the 1840s. Morris was also inspired by the social critic John Ruskin (1819–1900), whose attacks on the poor quality of mass-produced consumer products blamed industry for society's ills. Morris's own response was to instigate the first "design reprimand" of international influence, the Arts and Crafts Movement.

In 1861 Morris founded the design firm of Morris, Marshall and Faulkner, Fine Art Workmen in Painting, Carving, Furniture, and the Metals. Together with his collaborators and later followers, among them Charles Ashbee, William Burges, Charles Voysey, and Arthur Mackmurdo, Morris attempted a rebuttal against the tasteless design and shoddy construction of typical Victorian furniture. Carefully executing every detail of design, these artist-craftsmen produced only quality workmanship in good materials. But because hand-crafting was their sole and sovereign remedy for the present state of design as well as humanity in general, they did not recognize the machine's ultimate role. And, most unfortunately, they chose the Gothic historical style to communicate their ideas of reform.

As the movement matured, its limited scope became obvious. Handmade Arts and Crafts furniture was too expensive to be a marketable alternative to the machine's product. Consequently, the movement's dream of creating an art "for the people" was never realized. Morris himself eventually abandoned the "puristic" medieval styling for a more individualized interpretation.

Nevertheless, Morris's theories laid a constructive base for Contemporary furniture. His emphasis on the value of sound structure and the importance of the artist's role in the design of applied arts lived on. By the end of the century, craft schools and guilds were reestablished throughout England and the rest of Europe. Morris's presence would also be felt later in the foundation of the *Wiener Werkstätte*, the *Werkbund* movement, and the Bauhaus.

Art Nouveau: The Search for Modern Style

On the aesthetic side, the Art Nouveau designers of the late nineteenth and early twentieth centuries made a step in the right direction: They developed their own decorative style instead of pilfering from history. To some extent, they also employed new materials. But though Art Nouveau did not refute the machine, the extravagant, asymmetrical character of the new styling discouraged serial production.

The new trend focused on elongated lines in nature—insect feelers, flower stamens, slender stems, and leaves. Although nature was a traditional category of decoration, Art Nouveau played with it in a new way. Like European court styles as well as the previous Arts and Crafts style of Morris, Art Nouveau was a comprehensive decorative movement which provided a unified interior effect. Moreover, instead of existing exclusively as superficial ornaments, motifs frequently united with the furniture's basic form, making the line between structure and decoration indistinguishable. At a later date and in a more purified manner, the same statement can be made of classic Contemporary furniture.

The English Arts and Crafts affiliate, Arthur Mackmurdo (1851–1942), first expressed the "new art" in his book illustrations, furniture, and interiors of the 1880s. Yet despite its British conception, Art Nouveau made little innovative progress in Great Britain except for the revolutionary designs of Charles Rennie Macintosh (1868–1928).

During the early 1890s the Belgian Henry van de Velde imported and promoted the new style on the continent, where it was thoroughly investigated. Depending on the country, nature was realistically represented or stylized to the eventual point of abstraction. The most enthusiastic interpretations were the nightmarish, gothic contortions of the Spaniard Antonio Gaudí (1852–1926). More refined expressions were seen in the works of the Frenchmen Eugène Gaillard, Louis Majorelle, Hector Guimard, and Eugène Vallin, and their Belgian predecessors Victor Horta and van de Velde.

Van de Velde not only impressed this flamboyant side of Art Nouveau, but also was the guiding spirit of the more conservative approach taken by the central European countries. Josef Hoffmann, Koloman Moser, and Joseph Olbrich were major names associated with the Austrian version of Art Nouveau, the Vienna *Sezession.* Richard Riemerschmid, Hermann Obrist, and August Endell were well-known designers in the German Art Nouveau school referred to as *Jugendstil,* the "young style." These countries developed a more controlled strain of Art Nouveau and maintained their enthusiasm for its decorative exuberance for a shorter period of time.

By the early 1900s, progressive designers gradually found the decor of Art Nouveau no more appropriate for their age than the Gothic styling of William Morris four decades before. They began to realize that the key to Contemporary aesthetics was something more than selecting the right subject matter for motifs. Instead of concentrating on decoration, the design world soon confronted the crux of the matter: Why decorate at all? At the same time, designers reassessed the capabilities of the machine and the proper effects of those capabilities on its products' design. Those who continued in the Art Nouveau school later found themselves at a design impasse which terminated in the Art Deco style of the 1920s and 1930s. Meanwhile, in Austria and Germany, the stage was set for the appearance of Contemporary design.

Pre-World War I Design: Prelude to Contemporary Furniture

While concern for utilizing the machine seriously as a design tool gradually rose in Germany, the Austrians continued probing for a proper Contemporary aesthetic. The furniture of Josef Hoffmann (1870–1956) was the first to progress from the *Sezession's* Art Nouveau character to a more functional rectangular form.

Hoffmann, however, was not alone in formulating this smooth-surfaced style. A close affinity existed between his designs and the unorthodox Art Nouveau furnishings of the Scottish designer Charles Mackintosh. The two exchanged ideas when Mackintosh displayed his furnishings and interior styling at the *Sezession's* 1900 exhibition in Vienna. Then, in 1902, Hoffmann visited Mackintosh's Glasgow School of Art in Scotland, where Hoffmann was encouraged to start his own decorative workshop in Vienna the following year.

The *Wiener Werkstätte* (Vienna Workshops) was a unique combination of Arts and Crafts, Art Nouveau, and Hoffmann's own new design direction. As a decorative workshop in Morris's tradition, it was concerned with producing quality handcrafted products; everything from jewelry to bookbinding gained its attention. Unlike the Arts and Crafts movement in England, however, the *Werkstätte* ignored the traditional styling usually yoked to handcrafting. As with his previous *Sezession* designs, Hoffmann was still convinced of the need for a modern form of decoration. But instead of continuing the Art Nouveau preoccupation with nature, he believed that geometrical shapes—squares, rectangles, and circles—and neutral colors—such as black and white— were more legitimate motifs for modernization. These elements had never exclusively constituted an art movement before. Through the *Wiener Werkstätte,* Hoffmann's preference for abstract geometric form spread throughout Europe. For decades to come, this trend would direct the character of progressive design, though not as Hoffmann had originally intended. He placed less emphasis on the importance of decoration in applied art; but motifs, such as the square, still existed in his *Werkstätte* design.

Hoffmann not only found many allies in his new direction; he also had a staunch critic in his fellow countryman Adolf Loos (1870–1933). Loos demanded a more drastic purge of the decorative excess of the previous century than the lukewarmness of the *Wiener Werkstätte*. In articles published as early as 1897, Loos discredited designers who concerned themselves with a search for modern decorative styling, stating that ornamentation, not industrialization, was the root of the design world's problems. All decoration should be disregarded; beauty must be found in essential form alone.

Loos was not alone in this belief. By the time of the appearance of his most zealous manifesto, "Ornament and Crime," in 1908, the American Frank Lloyd Wright (1867–1959), the Austrian Otto Wagner (1841–1918), and the new breed of German industrial designers such as Richard Riemerschmid (1868–1957) had independently produced types of decoratively "nude" furnishings.

In Germany the turning away from surface ornamentation stemmed from the practical concern of designers, most of whom were architects and industrialists, for upgrading the standards of German consumer products. For the most part, manufactured goods were still at the low state of material quality and design found in the previous century. When in 1906 the German *Werkstätte* introduced machine furniture designed by Riemerschmid, adventurous manufacturers who were discontented with their own production, were pleased and, in the following year, began employing designers such as Peter Behrens (1868–1940) to direct their design programs. Also in 1907, Hermann Muthesius (1861–1927) founded the German *Werkbund* to further encourage interaction between the progressive artists and engineers of the day. Replacing the decorators of previous years, these designers were now able to exert their influence on mass-produced products.

In general, the *Werkbund* designers found their aesthetic direction to be in line with that of the Austrians. Their geometric styling and smooth surfaces were in tune with the Germans' views concerning the proper course of industrial styling. Muthesius, however, went further and encouraged fellow designers to design for and in the very spirit of the machine. This meant that standardization and modular designing should play a more important role in the future of design. The "typeforms" which Muthesius proposed disturbed those members of the *Werkbund* who strongly felt that his design stand would infringe on artistic creativity. This disagreement intensified, finally becoming a major topic at the *Werkbund* Congress of 1914, where Van de Velde, who had been the director of the Weimar Arts School (later reorganized and retitled *Staatlichen Bauhaus*) since 1902, was Muthesius's most outspoken opponent. But the controversy between uniformity and independent design expression was not settled there.

The outbreak of World War I in July of 1914 further delayed the resolution of the argument. Then, after the war, the validity of Muthesius's viewpoint became established. Postwar economics as well as the new art movements greatly favored his proposal for standardization. The de Stijl designers in particular, including Gerrit Rietveld (1888–1964) and Theo van Doesburg (1883–1931), supported the Rational position, thereby directly influencing the designers of the 1920s. The first bout, therefore, went to "machine aesthetics." But its advocates offered only the first of many other later interpretations for Contemporary furniture design.

Michael Thonet: The Exception

Surprisingly enough, however, in one notable instance in the nineteenth century these decades of soul-searching were bypassed, with results as valid as the designs of the 1920s: the Bentwood chairs of Michael Thonet.

In his own day, Thonet received princely approval and international endorsement from the Victorian design world. But this recognition centered around his earlier laminated designs and his more exclusive line of bentwood products, works which have little bearing today. Yet, at the same time as Morris's early attempts at design reform, Thonet's inexpensive utilitarian wares displayed the modern aesthetic of pure form. Except for a few random admirers, these classic designs passed into the twentieth century unappreciated.

But modern architects, disgusted with the available "decorator" furniture, not only considered them worthy of use in their interiors, but found guidelines for their own future designs in Thonet's marked simplicity. His descendants in the Thonet firm diversified to manufacture the early metal designs of such designers as Breuer, Stam, van der Rohe, and Le Corbusier. All of them substituted steel tubes for Thonet's bentwood in their attempts to capture the visual lightness of his half-century-old originals.

Thonet not only preceded these Rational designers, he surpassed them on one vital point: affordability. Evidenced in his simple form was proof of the logistics of mass production as well as the simple beauty and economy of validly used materials and honest construction. He blended all of these with his delightful design wit and invited his world to take a common, inexpensive, but truly extraordinary seat.

1

Michael Thonet (signature)

Michael Thonet

In the nineteenth century, Michael Thonet paved the way for classic Contemporary furniture. He developed the first assembly line mass production furniture process, an important facet of Contemporary design philosophy, and perfected two major construction techniques for Contemporary furniture design: molded plywood and bentwood. With the bentwood process he designed the earliest examples of furniture that we characterize as Contemporary classics.

Michael Thonet was born on July 2, 1796, in the Prussian (now West German) village of Boppard on the Rhine. His father, a cabinetmaker of Belgian descent, introduced him early in life to the art of traditional furniture making, apprenticing him in standard cabinet construction, veneering, and elaborate inlays.

Also inspiring Thonet's early development was David Roentgen (1743–1807). His well-known eighteenth-century furniture workshop had been located less than 20 kilometers away, in Neuwied. Though the quality and ingenious mechanical innovations of Roentgen's furniture placed it in great demand throughout the courts of Europe, particularly in France, his career was doomed, because the wealth of his clientele was depleted by the French Revolution. In 1795 Roentgen was forced to close his shop. On the other hand, success was assured Thonet because he was to produce furniture, which, because of its innovative construction, was more affordable and accessible to the world market.

Thonet began his professional career by establishing an independent cabinet shop in Boppard. The year was 1819. Though he specialized in marquetry and joinery, in 1830 he started to experiment in new furniture construction techniques: the molding of laminated veneers and the bending of solid rods—the bentwood technique. By 1836, he was able to form furniture from molded laminated sandwiches of thick veneers. His curved furniture therefore became cheaper, more durable, and lighter in weight than had been possible with the traditional solid-block carving technique. Realizing the significance of his laminated technique, Thonet applied for a patent in 1841 in Belgium, France, and England.

Later that year, the Chancellor of Austria, von Metternich (1773–1859), purchased some of Thonet's furniture after admiring it in a show in Coblenz. He convinced Thonet that establishing his workshop in Vienna would prove more profitable: after all, Vienna was the capital of the Hapsburg Empire and the cultural center of nineteenth-century Europe. To facilitate the move, the Chancellor provided the Thonet family the Imperial Cabinet Courier's coach.

Once in Vienna, Thonet met the Austrian Karl Leister, who in 1841 had established a factory for furniture production. In 1842 Thonet was granted the patent for his laminated process. Combining their resources in what would be a seven-year partnership, the two men spent five years helping to restore the Palace Liechtenstein in Vienna. This commission, under the direction of the Englishman P. H. Desvignes, afforded Thonet the opportunity to work further in his laminated process. Thonet also completed the development of the bentwood technique and produced the first group of chairs for the palace using the process. Leister and Thonet dissolved their partnership in 1849.

Then Thonet commercially applied the bentwood process on his own. Production began in a traditional Viennese cabinet shop established with Desvignes's financial backing. Both laminated and bentwood designs from this workshop were exhibited in the 1851 Crystal Palace Exhibition in London. Showing tables, chairs, sofas, and stands of rosewood and walnut, as well as inlaid flooring, Thonet was honored with an award of merit and thus became internationally recognized. Ironically, this recognition stemmed from his ornate Victorian designs and not the innovative process that produced them. His styling reflected the moods and values of the time: concealed structure with prettification through

applied motifs. Later, however, in order to create *billiger Konsumwaren*—inexpensive consumer products which were the hallmarks of Thonet's career—his total disregard for these traditional characteristics resulted in creative and original designs for machine production.

Tooling for Thonet's first factory for mass-producing bentwood furniture began in 1851. The equipment, which Thonet designed and built himself, was capable of bending rods of solid wood. This technique enabled him to produce furniture containing fewer parts and less material that was therefore lower in price than the laminated procedure from which it evolved. The factory became operational in Koritschan, Moravia (now Czechoslovakia), in 1856, and it antiquated the earlier workshop of master carpenters.

The earlier process had produced furniture of molded members built up from strips of thin wood veneers, saturated in warm glue, shaped in wooden molds, and cooled. Assembly took place after the parts were thoroughly dried and finished.

In contrast, the bentwood technique produced designs of solid rods. Suitable logs were divided into 30-mm (1⅛") square members. Lathing produced rods of the desired diameter and shape. After the required period of soaking and steaming, the softened rods were molded. Then, as with the laminated process, these parts were dried and finished. Except for the finishing and caning of seats and backs, this assembly line production was devoid of handcrafting.

Thonet laid a firm foundation for the ongoing success of the business in the two decades preceding his death in 1871. In 1852, his first European showroom opened in Vienna, followed by some 25 international showrooms including the 1853 opening on Broadway in New York. Thonet assured the continuity of the business when he transferred ownership to his sons on November 1, 1853. He changed the name of the firm to Gebrüder Thonet (Thonet Brothers) although he retained leadership, approving all new designs until his death. On July 10, 1856, Thonet received a patent for the bentwood technique which gave him a thirteen-year monopoly on the production of bentwood furniture. Constant demand for the furniture required a continual search for additional beechwood forests and eventually led to the planting of a large tract of land near Brno, Moravia (destroyed later by Hitler). Additional factories opened at Bystritz-am-Hostein in Germany, Grosz-Ugrocz in Hungary, Hallenhau in Russian Poland, and finally Frankenberg in Germany. When Thonet died on March 3, 1871, he left a vast empire and a worldwide demand for his furniture.

Thonet became the most successful furniture manufacturer in history. The twin properties of economy and function placed his furniture in demand. Due to the assembly line process, his furniture was inexpensive and competed well in a Victorian market bombarded with inferior products. No other designer of his day could claim to provide quality furniture at affordable prices.

To be sure, Thonet enjoyed immediate financial success with his product. But in terms of impact on the total scheme of furniture design, the historical significance of his procedures and styling was not realized for decades. His revolutionary technique was the basis of Alvar Aalto's two-dimensional molded plywood and laminated wood furniture of the 1930s, and of the more advanced three-dimensional work of Charles Eames in the 1940s. Complementing Thonet's technical achievements was his aesthetic contribution to Contemporary furniture design. His furniture embodied—in the mid-nineteenth century—the design principles that twentieth-century masters later came to value: material and construction honesty, with beauty dependent on form alone. This accomplishment inadvertently resulted from Thonet's process and his concern for low-cost quality, and not from the purely philosophical concerns which encumbered so many of the pre-World War I designers.

In the 1920s, however, designers increasingly began to recognize Thonet's impact. The Swiss architect Le Corbusier endorsed Thonet in 1925 when he explained the presence of Thonet's furniture in his architecture: "We have introduced the humble Thonet chair of steamed wood, certainly the most common as well as the least costly of chairs. And we believe that this chair, whose millions of representatives are used on the continent and in the two Americas, possesses nobility." But the highest compliment to the life and work of the pioneering Michael Thonet was the fact that Le Corbusier, as well as many other contemporary architects, continued to use Thonet's bentwood designs even after the development of his own furniture.

Design No. 14
(The Vienna Chair)

The oldest chair that deserves to be identified as a Contemporary classic is Michael Thonet's Model No. 14, commonly called the Vienna Chair. A product of the economical Thonet bentwood technique, it was introduced in 1859. The cost of the chair was astonishingly low: only three gulden, which in the 1850s was also the price of three dozen eggs. It has been estimated that over 40 million had been sold by 1900. The Vienna Chair is still in production today, and has become the most widely sold chair in history.

The chair was composed of six bentwood parts. Perhaps its most important innovation was the circular bent frame for the caned seat. Below the seat frame, a second circular rod acted as a stretcher. Slightly splayed rods formed the front legs, while a looped rod formed the back legs and back frame. A shorter loop added to the upper half of the back provided extra support. To secure the back, small curved braces were connected from each side of the back rest to the seat. In Europe, beechwood was used for all these pieces because it was readily available, economical, and easily adaptable to the bentwood process. Later, for the same reasons, elm was substituted in the American production models.

The chair was easily shipped "KD" (knocked down) and quickly assembled on site. After assembling, the Vienna Chair measured 400 mm (15¾") wide, 500 mm (19¹¹/₁₆") deep, and 880 mm (34⅝") high, with a seat height of 450 mm (17⅝").

Many variations of the prototype evolved. The fundamental seat frame was produced with more than 100 different back styles. Arms were incorporated. Wood seats, with or without upholstery, were substituted for the caning. Later, even settees were made in the basic style of the Vienna Chair.

During the more than 100 years in which the Vienna Chair has been in production, it has continued to be a popular and exciting expression of the innovative process that Michael Thonet invented and developed. Its open, linear simplicity has quietly but firmly established it as a Contemporary classic.

FIGURE 1

Design No. 14
(the Vienna Chair)

Bentwood Rocker

Michael Thonet introduced a curvilinear statement of movement, the Bentwood Rocker, in 1860. Its fluid lines and technical accomplishments have been admired for more than a century.

The origin of rocking chairs is a question of much controversy. Some records date the use of rockers as far back as 1762, when Eliakim Smith, a cabinetmaker and repairer in Hadley, Massachusetts, made notes which confirm that he had applied runners to ordinary cottage chairs. Records exist of rockers being in use in 1787 in the home of Benjamin Franklin. Other authorities claim that rockers were first conceived in England by the early designers of the English Windsor Chair in the late eighteenth century. In any event, examples of metal-framed rockers could be found in England and on the Continent by the mid-nineteenth century.

When Thonet exhibited his furniture in the Crystal Palace in 1851, he saw examples of these heavily tufted, clumsy rockers. Perhaps he was thus encouraged to add a rocker to his own line. But what influenced his design? The flowing, fluid lines of his rocking chair echo the rococo styling that Thonet had seen in the Palace Liechtenstein in Vienna. Too, he must have been mindful of the springs in carriage construction, for in the same year that his firm first produced the Bentwood Rocker, it also began to manufacture carriage wheels. Like all Thonet's bentwood furniture, his rocker was much lighter in scale and weight than preceding Victorian versions.

Acceptance of Thonet's Rocker has increased throughout the years. Most nineteenth-century furniture reflected the era's formal life-style. Because rockers connoted a more relaxed atmosphere, Europeans did not at first readily accept any rocker, especially Thonet's light, airy bentwood version. Throughout the rest of the world, however, it was used extensively, especially in areas with hot climates. A relaxed feeling in furniture was not only approved in these regions, it was demanded. Moreover, because the bentwood process eliminated the need for glue, the chairs proved more adaptable to climatic conditions. In contrast to the lack of initial enthusiasm in Europe, by the turn of the century more than 100,000 Bentwood Rockers were being purchased annually worldwide. Even for today's manufacturer, this is an astonishing volume.

Although the rocker appears at first glance complicated in form, Thonet constructed it from only eight parts which, as in his other designs, were screwed together. The supporting skeleton consisted of a comprehensive frame with stabilizing braces and stretchers. The frame formed the rocker's base and supported the arms, seat, and back. Since bentwood rods were not strong enough to be cantilevered, an undulating brace was added at each side to support the weight of the seat. A U-shaped stretcher stabilized the seat brace, while an oval brace was placed between the seat and the back. Stretchers were added to hold the sled bases parallel; these were the only straight elements in the entire design. The caning was attached onto bent rods outlining the seat and back, in a way similar to the caning of the Vienna Chair (Figure 1).

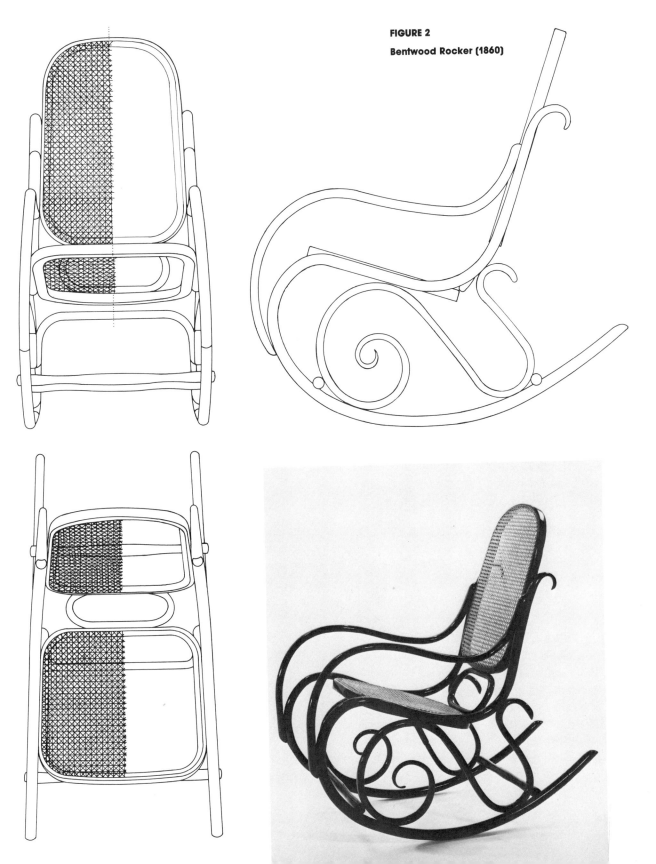

FIGURE 2
Bentwood Rocker (1860)

In overall dimensions the rocker was 550 mm (21⅝") wide, 950 mm (37⅜") deep, and 1,100 mm (43⅜") high, with a seat height of 460 mm (18⅛"). These proportions were such that even with its tall back, the rocker appeared horizontal in form.

The Bentwood Rocker has been the inspiration of many adaptations to its basic form. Over the years, Gebrüder Thonet continued to adapt and change the flow of the lines, creating dozens of different designs. One variation called for a bentwood rocking sofa with adjustable back. Another variation, which came in 1880, had a lower and more curvilinear shape, and more than likely influenced Le Corbusier's Chaise Longue (Figure 18). Thonet's designs also inspired Ludwig Mies van der Rohe's classic MR Chair (Figure 10) of 1926. The arms of the MR Chair and those of the Bentwood Rocker have a common denominator in their curve. And interestingly enough, Mies's chair was later manufactured by Gebrüder Thonet.

No other rocker has captured the spirit of rocking in its very form as has Thonet's. It remains a delightfully functional statement of classic furniture design.

Arm Chair No. 9
(The Le Corbusier Chair)

Gebrüder Thonet began production of Arm Chair No. 9 in 1870. Neither Michael Thonet nor his five sons could have dreamed then that fifty years later the Swiss architect Le Corbusier would endorse this product as an object capturing the *esprit nouveau* of the twentieth

century. Nor could they have forecast that over 100 years later, people would still be admiring, buying, and enjoying its simple elegance attained through technological perfection and purity.

Why did Le Corbusier select Arm Chair No. 9 over so many others? First, the chair was utilitarian: it served a function; it was a standard. Second, and equally important to Le Corbusier, the chair was appropriate to the times. Even though the design was fifty years old, its simplicity of line and construction as well as its honesty and clarity of materials devoid of surface decoration confirmed its kinship to the "new" movement. Arm Chair No. 9 was therefore an eminent answer to Le Corbusier's search for furniture which was compatible with his architectural aesthetic.

Arm Chair No. 9 had been a vast success even before being recognized by Le Corbusier, and was widely used in hospitals and cafes. However, it was when Le Corbusier selected the chair along with other Thonet furniture for use in the 1923 La Roche/Jeanneret Duplex in Paris that it gained acceptance in residential settings. Le Corbusier in fact used the chair often. In 1925 it received even more public attention and respect when it was shown in Paris in the pavilion of *L'Esprit Nouveau*, the structure Le Corbusier designed and built to show the world his new design concepts. (Today the building houses the *Fondation Le Corbusier*.) The chair was again specified in the interiors of Le Corbusier's entry into the 1927 Weissenhof Exhibition in Stuttgart and in his 1935 Weekend House in the suburbs of Paris. Today the chair appropriately bears Le Corbusier's

FIGURE 3

**Armchair No. 9
(The Le Corbusier Chair)**

name because he was particularly responsible for its later success.

The Le Corbusier Chair is indebted to earlier Thonet designs, especially to the Arm Chair No. 14 for its simple lines and basic concept. It simplified the earlier chair to only five elements: the rounded seat frame, the front legs, the rounded leg stretcher, the arc that forms the rear legs and back support, and the graceful rod that forms the arms and top of the back. Like all the bentwood furniture, the parts of Le Corbusier's chair could be shipped unassembled.

The chair's simplification was expressed in sensitive proportioning. The overall dimensions of the chair were: 430 mm (17") wide, 533 mm (21") deep, and 864 mm (34") high, with a seat height of 457 mm (18").

Le Corbusier summed up the qualities of the Arm Chair No. 9 when he described it as "humble," "common," and "noble." With this endorsement, he broadened the heritage of Michael Thonet's Arm Chair No. 9—the Le Corbusier Chair.

Design No. 18

A variation on the theme of an earlier Thonet Chair, Design No. 18, was introduced in 1876, five years after Michael Thonet's death. It was nevertheless an exemplary model of his Bentwood process.

Like Arm Chair No. 9, Design No. 18 contained only five parts: a rounded seat frame, two looped rods placed one inside the other to form the back legs and back support, the front legs, and a rounded stretcher. There

were at least four variations of the original stretcher; on some models the stretcher extended to provide lower support for the back legs. The overall dimensions of the chair were: 400 mm (15¾") wide, 500 mm (19¹¹⁄₁₆") deep, and 890 mm (35") high, with a seat height of 460 mm (18"). As with all of Thonet's Bentwood chairs, seats of caning, wood, and upholstery were produced.

Due to the nature of bentwood, light weight, durability, and inexpensiveness were inherent to Design No. 18. Its use as a lion tamer's chair since the late nineteenth century only reinforced its popularity. Because it was lightweight, the lion tamer could easily handle it; because it was sturdy and durable, it was strong enough to ward off the lion. If the lion did manage to get the best of the situation, replacing the chair would not necessitate securing a bank loan. Few chairs have so unique a claim to fame!

This popular Thonet design gained greater attention in the twentieth century when it was the point of discussion between two Contemporary architects: Adolf Loos and Le Corbusier. Corbusier favored Thonet's Bentwood Arm Chair No. 9 (Figure 3), although examples of the arm chair version of Chair No. 18 were also pictured in his La Rouche/Jeanneret residence in 1923. Loos preferred the side chair of Design No. 18. Although the two architects' disagreement was never resolved, their interest in Design No. 18 affirmed the chair's appropriateness to Contemporary architecture.

FIGURE 4
Design No. 18

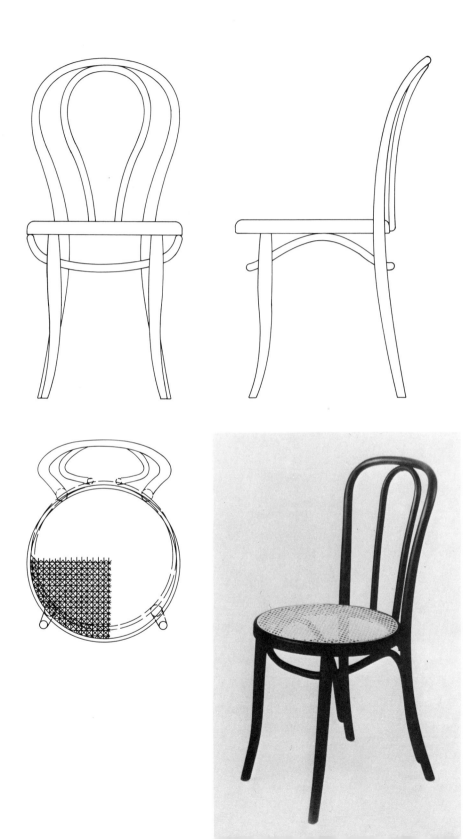

The International Style:
The Rational Furniture of the 1920s

Against the backdrop of postwar Europe, the first valid solution to our present-day furniture needs appeared. Along with the architecture to which it related, it later became popularly known as the "International Style," though its designers referred to it in a number of other ways: Puristic, Functional, Formal, Rational. Critics charged that it was cold, sterile, and inhumane. Of course, any innovation raises criticism. But regardless of the complaints, the new approach was the logical direction to follow. A clean break was made with the past, and a new aesthetic, suited to its historical situation, emerged.

Throughout Europe, life-styles had been permanently altered by the after-effects of World War I. Homes and families were smaller and were increasingly maintained without the assistance of servants. Construction materials, especially wood, were also limited and more costly than in prewar times. In this situation, the monumental, time-consuming hulks of furniture popular before the war were obviously no longer practical. Furniture was needed that was smaller, easier to maintain, and multifunctional.

Forward-thinking designers—abreast of technology and optimistic of its future—were sensitive to these developments. They blended the new artistic trends with industrial arts to meet the economic exigencies. The timing was right. They proposed their solutions and were accepted as the new avant garde.

Three men stand paramount among the multitude of designers of that time: Marcel Breuer, Mies van der Rohe, and Charles Edouard Jeanneret—Le Corbusier. Because of the interdependence and close communication within the design ambit of these men, many others influenced their work, and they in turn inspired countless others around the world with their revolutionary ideas.

Nationality was not an essential determinant in the success of these designers: van der Rohe was a German, Le Corbusier a Swiss living in Paris, and Breuer a Hungarian teaching at the Dessau Bauhaus. Much more important were the company they kept and the men they admired, such as Hoffmann, Loos, Wright, Muthesius, Behrens, and Rietveld. Likewise, previous design experience was not necessarily beneficial; in fact, it had hindered many of the precursors of these designers. The young designers of the 1920s attacked problems with open minds and could more freely articulate the solutions for a new day.

2

Marcel Breuer (signature)

Marcel Breuer

The architect Marcel Breuer is popularly known for having initiated one of the most influential breakthroughs in the development of Contemporary furniture: While a Master of the Bauhaus, he designed the first chair for interiors using tubular steel. This was the first classic furniture of the twentieth century. The year was 1925, and Breuer was only 23 years old. So ideally did this material fulfill the needs of the time that it was instantly recognized and utilized by major European furniture designers: Stam, Mies, Le Corbusier, Perriand, Roth, and Aalto, to name only a few. Equal in impact to this triumphant debut, however, was Breuer's open-mindedness toward the use of any material throughout more than fifty years of designing both furniture and architecture.

Marcel Lajos Breuer was born in the Danube valley town of Pécs in southern Hungary, the son of a local doctor. During Breuer's early years he developed an interest in painting and sculpture which resulted in a scholarship to study at the Viennese Academy of Fine Art. So, in the fall of 1920, at age 18, Breuer set out for Vienna, the nearest large city and a hub of culture at the time. He was so excited, he actually walked there.

But Breuer stayed in Vienna only five weeks. After investigation, the curriculum of the Beaux-Arts Academy no longer appealed to the young man. So, instead of pursuing fine art, Breuer redirected his artistic talent into the more practical career of architecture, beginning with an apprenticeship in the local workshop of the architect Hans Bolek. Once again he encountered problems. Unsure of how to use even the most elementary construction tools, he forced a new blade into a wood planer with a hammer, then left in embarrassment. This setback disappointed but did not discourage Breuer. He now realized that he must start from the bottom to acquire the practical fundamentals which his background had not provided. Through a Hungarian friend, Fred Forbat, he heard of the Bauhaus school in Weimar, Germany, and they both enrolled.

As a student in the formative Weimar Bauhaus of the early 1920s, Breuer was exposed to every major Contemporary art movement, the most influential being Expressionism, de Stijl, and Constructivism. Various proponents of these styles in the Bauhaus created discord within the school. Johannes Itten (1888–1967), who taught the preliminary design course from

1918 to 1923, directed the Bauhaus toward Expressionism. The addition of the Abstract Expressionists Paul Klee (1879–1940) in 1921 and Wassily Kandinsky (1866–1944) in 1922 reinforced Itten. In 1922, however, a conflict arose. Theo van Doesburg (1883–1931), an advocate of the rational directions of the modern art movements, de Stijl and Constructivism, lectured at the Bauhaus and later established a competitive school in Weimar. His luring of students from the Bauhaus led to conflicts in the staff and the student body concerning the Bauhaus's direction. As a result, when Itten departed in 1923, Breuer, as well as the Bauhaus in general, gradually shed Expressionistic tendencies. This change of attitude was encouraged by Laszlo Moholy-Nagy (1895–1946), who replaced Itten in 1923 and began teaching the primary design course. Throughout all the confusion the head of the Bauhaus, Walter Gropius, allowed teachers and students total freedom of affiliation to the various movements as long as they concentrated on his original objective of training both hand and mind.

Breuer was an exceptional student, and in this restless atmosphere he was encouraged to experiment and to assimilate his own concepts of design. He particularly excelled in furniture design to the point that by April 1925, when the Nazi Party forced the Bauhaus to move from Weimar to the nearby industrial city of Dessau, Breuer was no longer a student: he was a Master of the Bauhaus. With the move to Dessau, Breuer took over leadership of the carpentry and furniture workshop and accepted the responsibility of furnishing the new Bauhaus facility and seven faculty residences, all designed by Gropius. This commission resulted in the first tubular steel furniture intended for general use: the Wassily Chair (Figure 5), the Laccio Stool/Table (Figure 6), auditorium seating, and various other furniture pieces. The completion date for the residences was the summer of 1926, and the new facilities officially opened in December 1926.

In 1927, Breuer left the Bauhaus to pursue architecture and continue in his furniture design. Because there were few design opportunities in Dessau beyond an occasional interiors commission, in the spring of 1928, he opened an office in Berlin. In the ensuing depression and political climate, architectural commissions were few in Germany, even in Berlin. Therefore, Breuer concentrated on interiors. Fortunately, he received royalties from his furniture designs, which were being manufactured by Gebrüder Thonet.

In 1931, Breuer was able to make a travel/lecture tour through Europe and northern Africa. These travels proved extremely influential in personalizing Breuer's earlier Rational architectural approach. He was impressed with the construction of ships and its applicability to architecture. And, like so many others, he recognized the simplicity and honesty of vernacular houses. Breuer was particularly fascinated with their play of textures and light and their intriguing combinations of materials. All aspects of these observations were eventually incorporated into his mature architectural style.

Finally, in 1932, Breuer received his first architectural commission: the Harnischmacher's residence in Wiesbaden, Germany. In 1933, at the request of Sigfried Giedion, he was involved in another commission: He collaborated with E. and A. Roth in designing the Dolderhal Apartments in Zurich. But in 1935 Breuer left Berlin for London to escape the growing political pressures of the Third Reich.

Once in London, Breuer entered into an architectural partnership with F. R. S. Yorke. Their most outstanding work was the Bristol Pavillion, which displayed features to be found in Breuer's later work: contemporary spatial concepts and structure, not necessarily limited to modern materials. In 1937 Walter Gropius invited Breuer to join him in teaching at Harvard University and to establish an architectural partnership in Cambridge, Massachusetts. Together, Breuer and Gropius became pacesetting residential architects, introducing traditional materials into the Modern Movement. The Chamberlain Cottage (1940) in Weyland, Massachusetts, was an outstanding product of this period.

After termination of this partnership in 1941, Breuer remained at Harvard until he opened his own architectural office in New York City in 1946. His firm grew into international size, receiving large architectural commissions that included the UNESCO Buildings in Paris, 1953–1958 (in collaboration with the Italian engineer Nervi and the French architect Zehrfuss); the Whitney Museum in New York City, 1963–1966; and the Research Center of IBM in La Gaude, France, 1962. In the summer of 1977, Breuer, 75 years old, retired from active daily participation in his architectural office. He died on July 1, 1981.

Breuer's early student furniture designs often utilized molded wood and plywood. By 1924, he had designed and constructed numerous chairs, tables, desks, beds, and modular storage units. Although some of this furniture displayed obvious Expressionistic tendencies, his composition progressed toward a lightweight geometric form. While mimicking the de Stijl look of Gerrit Thomas Rietveld (1888–1964), Breuer's chairs reflected his own interest in human comfort: resilient frames, curved seat and chair backs, and stretched fabric upholstery. Van Doesburg took note of this deviation from pure de Stijl styling and condemned it as early as 1922, but Breuer remained steadfast in his concern for comfort. His mature furniture style surfaced: rational composition with humanizing aspects of the Expressionists.

Approximately thirty of Breuer's designs were shown in the 1930 Gebrüder Thonet catalog, including the Bauhaus designs, the Cesca Chair (Figures 7 and 8), the Breuer Lounge Chair (Figure 9), tea carts, dining tables, and folding chairs—all of tubular steel. After exploiting this material, Breuer continued to investigate other furniture materials, particularly aluminum and molded plywood. Applying the spring characteristics of aluminum, Breuer branched into this new material in 1933 in his continuing search for comfortable furniture. That same year, he entered the international Parisian competition for aluminum furniture with an elegant collection of tables, lounges, and arm and side chairs. Even though he won first prize from both the jury of designers and the jury of industrialists, his designs were manufactured for only a short period.

Breuer returned to using plywood in 1935, substituting it for the frame of his earlier aluminum furniture. These pieces were manufactured in England in association with Jack Pritchard, head of Isokon Furniture. Breuer had recognized and appreciated the capacities of wood during his experimentations at the Bauhaus, and had even incorporated it in some of the first furniture using tubular steel (the Laccio Stool/Table and the Cesca Chair). For Isokon, he designed the Breuer Plywood Lounge Chair as well as stacking plywood chairs, arm chairs, and nesting tables. When he moved to America in 1937, he continued to work in plywood. In 1945, he designed "cutout" furniture in an attempt to produce thrifty plywood furniture that minimized the waste in production. After 1946, Breuer concentrated more heavily on his architecture, although he did occasionally design custom furniture for specific jobs.

Throughout his career Marcel Breuer rarely discounted an old material simply because it was old. Nor did he exalt a new material simply because it was new. Rather, he used old and new elements in a functional, aesthetic, and honest manner. Both his furniture and architecture confirm this fact. To Breuer, any material, new or old, had a place in the contemporary environment if properly understood and handled.

Wassily Chair

In 1925 Marcel Breuer designed the Wassily Chair, the first chair for interior use constructed of tubular steel. Its courageous and honest use of materials, its sensitive proportioning, and its innovative technical qualities have made it one of today's best-known twentieth-century classics.

FIGURE 5
The Wassily Chair

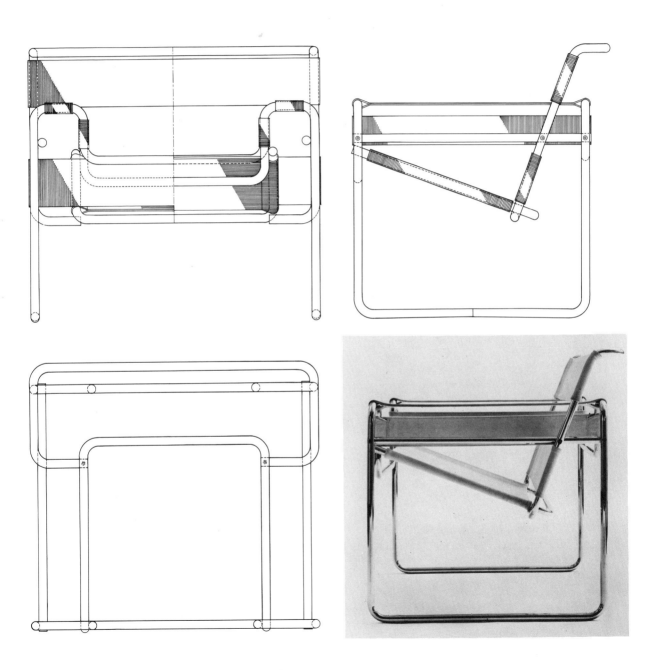

The Wassily Chair was the first piece of furniture Breuer designed for the provocative Dessau Bauhaus buildings. Bearing on its design were all the influences that he had encountered at the Bauhaus: the boxy shape from the Cubists, the composition of intersecting planes from the de Stijl, and the exposed and complicated skeletal framework from the Constructivists. By means of these influences, Breuer introduced a new material—tubular steel.

Though the chair was the first to specify tubular steel for general interior use, it was neither the first piece of furniture using metal nor the first piece of furniture using tubular steel. Iron-based rockers and metal children's beds have prevailed in many mid-nineteenth-century interiors. Edouard Manet, in his Parisian garden settings, painted hundreds of iron-framed chairs. Soon after the Mannesmann Steel Works developed the first seamless tubular steel rod in 1886, tubular steel hospital beds were manufactured. In 1925 Le Corbusier used tubular steel for the legs of the cabinets in the pavilion of *L'Esprit Nouveau* in Paris. That same year, Breuer recognized the material as symbolic of modern technology, which he found so fascinating. Tubular steel's light weight, affordability, durability, bendability, and sanitary finish made it the most appropriate material for his new chair.

Not everyone agreed with Breuer. When the young designer approached the Adler Bicycle Works to get them to produce the frames (he had first conceived of the appropriateness of tubular steel when riding his new and, interestingly enough, *first* bicycle—an Adler), they thought he was drunk, arguing that no one would want a chair made of *that* material in a home. Still determined, he turned to a local Dessau pipe fitter, who made the first chair.

The original Wassily Chair consisted of a skeleton of 20 mm ($1\frac{3}{16}$") steel tubes which defined the Cubist shape without containing it. These tubes formed the leg frame and structural supports for the seat and back. Canvas strategically stretched over this skeleton ensured that the user's body never came in direct contact with the steel. The two pieces of tubular steel composing the leg frame were each bent in eight places and connected in the middle to form the two sled bases. Near the top of the leg frame on each side of the chair, running from front to back, a crossbar was placed to brace the leg frame and provided a point of attachment for the back. The back supports attached to the crossbars at a sloping angle. A U-shaped seat frame rested on the back supports and attached to the front legs. Screws secured these attachments. The open ends of the tubes were capped and polished to a matching finish. Two canvas strips on each side of the leg frame, one horizontal and the other vertical, formed the arms; these strips penetrated the two canvas strips of the back. A single width of stretched upholstery formed the seat.

The dimensions of the chair were: 780 mm (30¾") wide, 685 mm (27") deep, and 725 mm (28½") high, with a seat height of 430 mm (17") and an arm height of 600 mm (23¾").

Variations from the original design occurred in both the frame and the upholstery. By 1930, when Thonet began to manufacture the chair, chrome plating—brighter in finish and not prone to tarnishing—had replaced nickel plating. The shape of the frame varied slightly as well. As pictured in Thonet's 1930 catalog, Model B3 incorporated a bracing bar on the floor that ran from side to side of a slightly arched sled base. Seat and leg frames were incorporated into one frame. A U-shaped frame replaced the back supports and became a permanent feature of the chair. Leather, an alternative to the canvas, appeared at this time as well. In spite of these variations, however, the character of the original Wassily Chair was not lost.

The chair became known as the "Wassily Chair" in the 1950s when Gavina of Milan introduced it to their line under that name. The name honored Breuer's colleague and friend at the Bauhaus, Wassily Kandinsky, in whose residence the first chair reportedly was used.

The impact of the Wassily Chair was overwhelming. Its daring use of tubular steel affected not only Breuer's later work, but also the work of hundreds of other furniture designers. Its form was also influential. In 1928 Le Corbusier, besides using tubular steel for his furniture, was directly influenced by the basic format of the Wassily Chair in designing his famous Basculant Chair (Figure 22). But most important was the Wassily Chair's historical significance: it was the first dynamic, innovative classic to appear in the twentieth century.

Laccio Stool/Table

In 1925 Marcel Breuer designed the Laccio Stool/Table as part of his collection of furniture for the Dessau Bauhaus. Like the Wassily Chair, the Laccio Stool/Table was made of tubular steel. Moreover, it was a forerunner of the cantilever principle in furniture design.

There is great controversy over who was the initial "discoverer" of the cantilever principle in furniture design. While working on the Bauhaus commission, Breuer reportedly once turned his Laccio Stool/Table on its side and remarked to the visiting Dutch architect Mart Stam that this was the basis of his next chair—a cantilevered design. In 1926 Stam produced a cantilevered chair made of straight lengths of plumbing pipe and elbow joints; supposedly, he had been working on this chair for several years. That same year, Mies van der Rohe, who knew of Stam's cantilevered chair, altered its basic shape and thus arrived at the first *resilient* cantilevered chair—the MR Chair (Figure 10). Finally, in 1928, Breuer designed his own version of the cantilevered chair—the Cesca Chair (Figure 7), based on his Laccio Stool/Table.

The simple appearance of the stool/table reflected structural honesty, Breuer's goal in all his furniture. Its frame was bent in eight places. Then a wooden top, stained black, was simply screwed into place.

Originally, the stool/table was made in four different sizes, whose measurements were as follows: 350 mm (13¾") wide, 350 mm (13¾") deep, and 450 mm (17⅝") high; 450 mm (17⅝") wide, 350 mm (13¾") deep, and 500 mm (19¹¹⁄₁₆") high; 560 mm (22") wide, 350 mm (13¾") deep, and 600 mm (23⅝") high; and 490 mm (19⅜") wide, 350 mm (13¾") deep, and 550 mm (21⅝") high.

This piece of furniture was very versatile, serving as both a stool and a table. There were at least sixty used as stools in the Bauhaus canteen. (Gropius's ingenious plan for the Bauhaus buildings separated the auditorium and canteen by a common stage. Thus, the canteen basically became an overflow space for lectures and special events.) The piece was intended for occasional use as a table as well. Many photographs of the Bauhaus interior confirm this usage—notably in the masters' homes and in theatre productions, in which the table was often pictured as a prop.

With all its versatility, the Laccio Stool/Table has undergone very few variations. As on all Breuer's furniture produced at this time, the original nickel plating had changed to chrome plating by 1930. Even though Breuer later substituted glass for variety, the design is still available in its original wooden top.

The Laccio Stool/Table received its name in the 1950s from Gavina, its manufacturer at the time. It stems from the Italian spelling of Marcel Breuer's middle name, Lajos. The name continues to be used today.

The Laccio Stool/Table was a clear, honest, and practical statement of Contemporary design. It proved Breuer's belief that only through simplicity can furniture be versatile enough to adapt to the multifaceted activities of modern living.

FIGURE 6
The Laccio Stool/Table

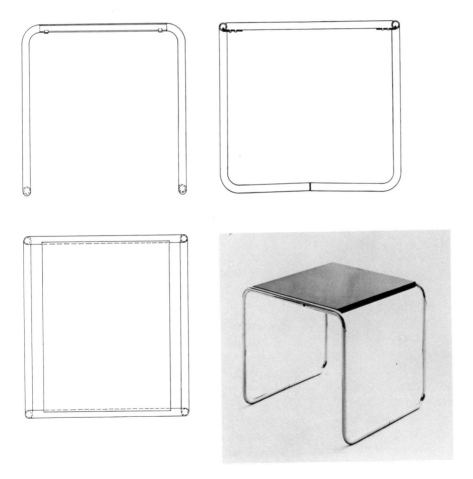

Cesca Chair

The Cesca Chair, named after Marcel Breuer's daughter, Cheska, was his contribution to the field of cantilevered chairs. Although it was not the first chair designed on this principle the Cesca Chair is the design normally associated with the terms "cantilever" and "tubular steel."

With the Cesca Chair, Breuer continued his exploration into the use of tubular steel as a suitable framing material, and furthered his belief that new and old materials could be successfully handled in an aesthetic relevant to our time. The sled base and support for the seat, back, and arm rests was bent from a single length of steel tubing. The seat and the back consisted of bent wooden frames, filled with natural caning and secured to the metal support with screws. The successful combination of these materials resulted in a chair of straightforward and puristic composition.

Incorporated in this simple design was Breuer's concern for human comfort. Its caning added to the resiliency found when tubular steel is cantilevered. The introduction of the wooden frames and arm rests, which prevented direct contact with the tubular steel, further assured comfort. The slight downward turn of the front edge of the seat made prolonged sitting more comfortable.

The dimenions of the side chair were 463 mm (18¼") wide, 575 mm (22⅝") deep, and 800 mm (31½") high, with a seat height of 463 mm (18¼"). The chair also was available in an arm chair that measured 575 mm (22⅝") wide, 575 mm (22⅝") deep, and 800 mm (31½") high, with a seat height of 463 mm (18¼") and an arm height of 692 mm (27¼").

As mentioned previously, the question of influence arises when discussing the history of cantilevered chairs. Breuer's Cesca Chair appeared after designs of Mart Stam and Mies van der Rohe. But who influenced whom? Each designer knew of the other's work. However, the design of Breuer's chair stemmed from his earlier Laccio Stool/Table which he designed in 1925. Mart Stam was at the same time involved with making a camping chair for his wife with an angular cantilevered base—technically the "first" executed cantilevered chair. Stam's chair appeared two years before Breuer's Cesca Chair, and indeed, it mimicked the Laccio Stool/Table on its side. Regardless of the influence, however, Breuer's Cesca Chair improved and refined Stam's original chair to an acceptable level of marketable quality. Interestingly enough, a chair designed by Stam which is almost identical to the Cesca Chair is manufactured and well known in Europe.

As with all Breuer's furniture, major variations have occurred in the fifty-year history of the Cesca Chair. A wider variety of finishes and materials is available today: Either handwoven or machine-woven caning, natural lacquer finishes on beech and oak as well as the original ebony finish, and upholstery versions with an upholstery arm rest or the original wooden arm rest. These minor variations have increased the chair's applicability to a wider number of situations and interiors.

With Breuer's blending of steel, wood, and cane, the spartan cantilever principle assumed a sensitive new form. The Cesca Chair further matured the initial concepts of Breuer's Bauhaus furniture and became equally, if not more, influential in the history of Contemporary furniture.

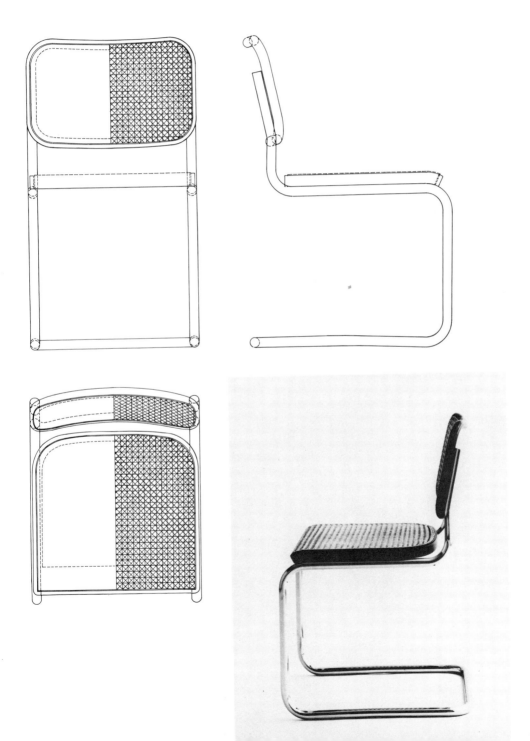

FIGURE 7
The Cesca Side Chair

FIGURE 8
The Cesca Arm Chair

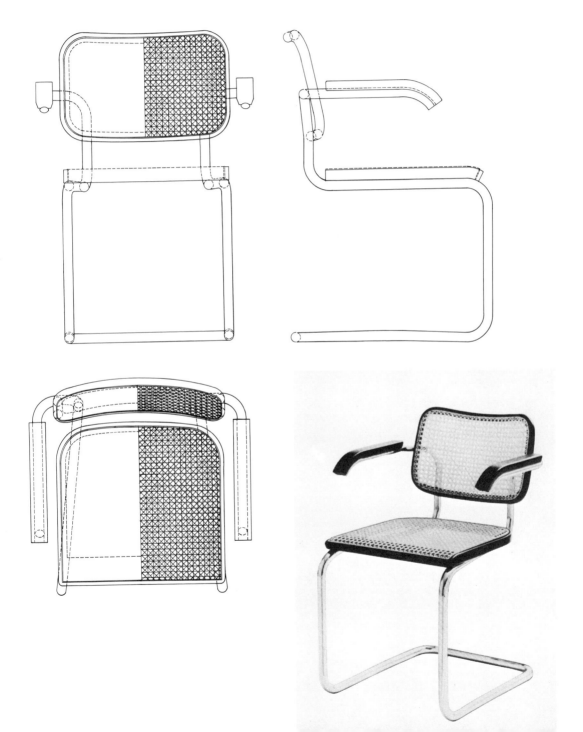

Breuer Lounge Chair

When Marcel Breuer established the use of tubular steel in furniture design in 1925, he sought lightness coupled with comfort. Stam and Mies soon followed with their own contributions: the first cantilevered chair and the first resiliently cantilevered chair. Breuer himself designed his own resilient cantilevered chair, the Cesca Chair (Figures 7 and 8), in 1928. But he realized that up to this point the principle had only been applied to upright seating. So in 1929, once again using tubular steel, Breuer designed a lounge chair that exploited the resiliency of the cantilever principle as none had before.

Breuer's Lounge Chair was totally resilient. In contrast to Mies's MR Chair (Figure 10), both the arms and the seat were cantilevered from the same bent tubular frame. (In Breuer's own Cesca Chair the arms were cantilevered but rigid.) In Breuer's typical Cubist form, the seat was placed lower and at an angle that positioned the weight of the body considerably back in the chair. Therefore, the spring characteristics of the tubular steel were more easily triggered and the chair was more resilient. The arm, a floating extension of the frame, captured this same degree of resiliency.

Breuer's concern for comfort was not limited to his use of resiliency; it was also very evident in his choice and placement of upholstery for the lounge chair. As the first designer to use tubular steel, Breuer was also the first to realize that this material was cold to the touch. From the beginning he always provided his tubular steel furniture with some material that would buffer the user's body from this coldness. In the Wassily Chair (Figure 5) it was canvas or leather; in the Cesca Chair (Figures 7 and 8) it was wood and cane. The Breuer Lounge Chair eventually incorporated materials that ranged from canvas to continuous caning to leather and pony skin. These coverings were placed on the seat and back. Wood capped the arms in such a way that it was never necessary for the body to come into direct contact with the cold metal.

Breuer designed three versions of the Lounge Chair: one with padded upholstery, one with a sling upholstery, and one with continuous caning. Examples of the padded version were first seen in Berlin in the De Francesco apartment, which Breuer designed in 1929. The sling version was soon available and was pictured as Model No. 35 in Gebrüder Thonet catalogs dating back to the early 1930s. The caned version followed soon after. The frames of these chairs differed slightly: the padded version showed no bracing on the frame, whereas the frames of the sling and cane versions had a tube that braced the back legs near the floor.

Only the sling and caned versions remain in production today. They continue to have the bracing bar, though it is now attached near the top of the back. Additional braces are also found under the seat of today's models.

The chair measures 650 mm (25⅝") wide, 800 mm (31½") deep, and 825 mm (32½") high, with a seat height of 370 mm (14½").

Marcel Breuer successfully combined the use of tubular steel and the resilient cantilever principle in an extremely simple, lightweight, comfortable lounge chair. Its continued popularity confirms Breuer's decision that such a lounge chair could function in the contemporary environment.

FIGURE 9

The Breuer Lounge Chair

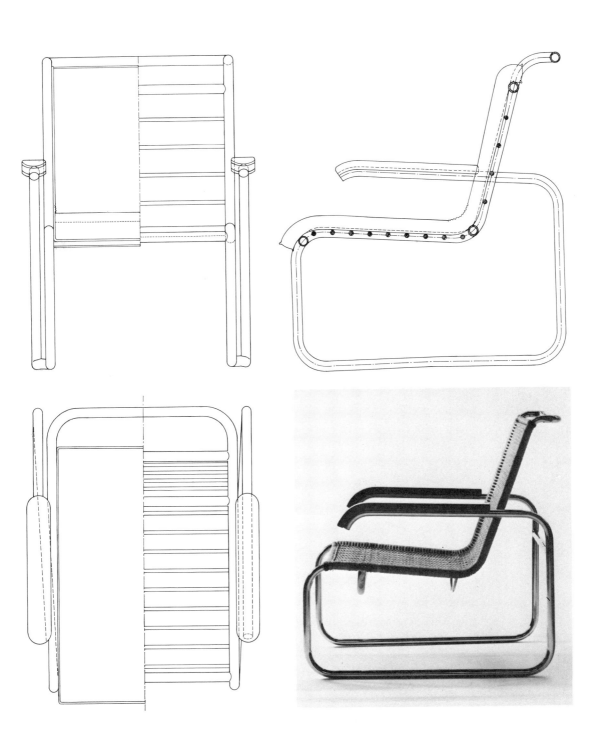

3

Ludwig Mies van der Rohe

One of the pioneers of modern architectural and furniture design was Ludwig Mies van der Rohe. Although he was basically considered an architect, his furniture work also had a dynamic and innovative impact. Abounding in structural honesty and clarity, his work displays an outstanding awareness of proportion, impressive detailing, faultless craftsmanship, and richness and integrity of materials. His pure, simple design concepts, at once functional and formal, furthered the acceptance of the Contemporary movement.

Ludwig Mies—who added his mother's maiden name, van der Rohe, in his twenties—was born on March 27, 1886, in Aachen, Germany (Aix-la-Chapelle), which is located in the province of North Rhineland-Westphalia bordering Belgium and Holland. This medieval city first gave him an awareness and appreciation of architecture. Its ancient buildings, though over a thousand years old, possessed qualities of simplicity and durability that he would later seek in his own work.

Working with his father in the family stone-masonry shop, Mies learned the properties and manipulable possibilities of stone as well as a respect for craftsmanship. Though he later worked with other materials—predominantly glass and metal—he was better able to understand their qualities as a result of these boyhood discoveries.

Mies's formal education began in the cathedral school founded in Aachen by Charlemagne in the ninth century, and ended after two years of trade school. When Mies was 15, his father, who had earlier recognized the innate drafting skills of his son, began apprenticing Mies to different local architects. In 1905 an Aachen architect persuaded Mies to complete his training in the more progressive city of Berlin. He worked for two years as a draftsman for Berlin's leading cabinetmaker, Bruno Paul (1874–1968), and completed six apprenticeships by 1907.

After this period of apprenticeship, Mies received his first commission, to build a residence in Berlin-Neuabelsberg. Before he began the work, his client, Dr. Riejl, sent him to Italy to study classical design, where he observed in particular the Pitti Palace and the Roman ruins. Mies's traditionally oriented residence was faultlessly executed—an extraordinary fact when one considers that he was only 21 years old.

Events from 1908 to 1912 proved the most influential to Mies's design philosophy. During this period he worked under the progressive German architect Peter Behrens (1868–1940) in Berlin and was also exposed to the innovative architecture of Hendrik Petrus Berlage (1856–1934) in The Hague. Both experiences reinforced his consciousness of craftsmanship and his understanding of the nature of materials. Most important, this early exposure to the theories and characteristics of the incipient Modern movement gave Mies's design concepts new direction.

Behrens's impact on Mies's work can be better understood when one considers that also working in Behrens's office were both Walter Gropius and Le Corbusier. In Berlin the young Mies was exposed to a wide and impressive range of influences. He obtained a practical knowledge of the capabilities of modern materials and of construction techniques. Like other architects at this time, including Behrens, he began to reflect the influences of Karl Friedrich Schinkel (1781–1841) in his work. He extracted the simple formality and sense of proportion of this Neoclassical architect and interpreted them to fill the needs of the twentieth century. While working with Behrens, Mies also first came into contact with the open planning and spatial concepts of Frank Lloyd Wright, whose work was exhibited in Berlin in 1910.

The following year Mies left Behrens and stayed for a year in Holland, where he studied the work of Berlage. This Dutch architect worked in traditional materials, but stressed in his designs that these materials be used honestly. With his simplified neoclassicism, he reintroduced flat, smooth walls to twentieth-century architecture at a time of Victorian chaos. These major influences on Mies's early life are easily recognizable in his architecture and furniture-design careers.

After World War I the atmosphere in Berlin nurtured many art movements which left their impression on architecture and furniture. Among these were Russian Constructivism, which placed emphasis on space rather than mass, and the de Stijl movement from Holland, which simplified and clarified form and line. In the late 1920s the National Socialist Party stifled much of this creativity which had surfaced in the Weimar Republic.

But in spite of the rise of Nazism, this was a productive period for Mies van der Rohe. As vice-president of the German *Werkbund,* in 1927 Mies opened the Weissenhof Housing Settlement in Stuttgart. This group of buildings displayed the work of major modern European architects. Mies himself executed a four-story apartment complex. In these interiors the resiliently cantilevered MR Chair (Figure 10) was first shown. Its design was influenced by the work in the cantilever principle of the Dutch designer Mart Stam (1899–   ) and the pioneering work in the use of tubular steel for furniture of the Hungarian Marcel Breuer. Two years later, in 1929, in collaboration with Lilly Reich (1885–1947), Mies produced a second chair—the Barcelona (Figure 11)—for the German Pavilion at the International Exhibition in Barcelona, Spain.

The Tugendhat Residence (1930) in Brno, Czechoslovakia, was Mies's next architectural project. For it, he designed the Brno Chair (Figure 14), the Tugendhat Chair (Figure 13), and a low X-based Table (Figure 16), all reminiscent of the earlier Barcelona designs.

(During World War II, the Tugendhat Residence was used as a stable and was badly damaged. Today, as a gift of the Tugendhat family, the building is used as a children's clinic.) In 1930 Mies also designed his famous Couch (Figure 17) for the New York City apartment of Philip Johnson. That same year Mies moved to Dessau, Germany (now East Germany), to become director of the now famous Bauhaus School, a post which his predecessors, Walter Gropius and Hannes Meyer, had resigned due to political pressure. Finally the Nazi Party forced the school to move to Berlin in 1932. After convincing the local Gestapo to allow the school to remain open, Mies, as a gesture of defiance, closed the Bauhaus on April 12, 1933.

Mies continued his architecture in Berlin, concentrating on residential designs, but due to Nazi opposition to Modern design principles he received few commissions. During this period his livelihood was dependent on royalties earned from the sale of his furniture, which was gaining in popularity outside Germany. In 1937, a residential commission from Mr. and Mrs. Stanley B. Resor for their home in Jackson Hole, Wyoming, brought Mies to the United States for the first time. For several years, a Chicago architect, John A. Holabird, had been trying to persuade him to become the director of the school of architecture of Armour Institute. (Armour Institute merged with Lewis Institute in 1940 to become The Illinois Institute of Technology.) But it was not until 1938 that Mies was prepared to leave Germany.

Shortly after Mies arrived to head the school of architecture of Armour Institute, the president of the institute, Henry T. Heald, awarded him the commission to design the master plan for the campus. Even with a limited knowledge of English, Mies conveyed to his students his rational approach to architecture and the need for complete mastery of architectural skills. And in turn, teaching forced Mies to clarify his own ideas on architecture.

But during his twenty-year affiliation with the school, Mies's activities were not limited to teaching; he continued his private practice of architecture and furniture designing. In 1946 he experimented with one-piece molded plastic chairs which he called "Conchoidal." Dozens of sketches were produced, but the furniture was not realized because the proposed techniques and materials were too costly for production at that time. It was not until the 1960s that Verner Panton (1926–   ) finally succeeded in producing furniture of this kind. In 1951 Mies designed the influential Lakeshore Drive Apartment towers in Chicago. He resigned in 1958 from IIT to devote full time to his architectural practice, and in collaboration with Philip Johnson designed the Seagram Building in New York City. Other outstanding architectural works include the Farnsworth House in Plano, Illinois (1950); the Barcardi Office near Mexico City (1961); and the New National Gallery in Berlin (1963). His practice continued until his death on August 17, 1969.

Like other Contemporary architects, Mies began to design furniture because he was unable to find furniture designs that complemented his architecture. Each piece embodied his own individual sense of proportion, formality, and simplicity and his own particular awareness of details. The designer's ample physique was reflected in the scale of his furniture. A man interested in quality and in detail, he always wore hand-tailored suits and enjoyed the finest of wines. But though his life-style was sophisticated, it was also simple. This simplicity could be seen in his Chicago apartment at 200 East Pearson, where limited use of his furniture emphasized the individual beauty of each piece and proclaimed his famous motto: "Less is more."

MR Chair

Mies van der Rohe began designing the MR Chair in 1926 and exhibited both arm and side chair versions in his model apartments at the 1927 Weissenhof Exhibition in Stuttgart. Later that year, the MR Chair was shown once again at the "Velvet and Silk Cafe" of the *Exhibition de la Mode* in Berlin. The chair not only reflected Mies's distinguished formal approach to design; more importantly, it represented the first success in resiliently cantilevered tubular steel furniture.

The influences in Mies's use of the cantilever principle and tubular steel, as well as in the overall form of the MR Chair, are easy to trace. In 1925 Marcel Breuer introduced tubular steel to general interior use in his Wassily Chair (Figure 5). Mies, like other designers, quickly recognized the compatibility of this revolutionary material with the Contemporary design ethos. And, while preparing for the Weissenhof Exhibition, Mies met Breuer himself. By 1926, Mart Stam had designed the first cantilevered chair—an awkward construction of plumbing pipes and joints designed to be easily dismounted and transported. Stam was unable to translate his designs into the more

refined look of continuous tubular steel, for he lacked technicians. Mies, however, had technicians at his disposal. After learning of the work of these two important furniture designers, Mies went on to design his own tubular steel cantilevered chair.

The form of Mies's cantilevered tubular steel chair was reminiscent of furniture designs more than sixty years old. The front curves of the MR Chair strongly resembled the lines of tubular-iron rockers designed in Europe during the mid-nineteenth century and those of the Bentwood Rocker (Figure 2) designed by Michael Thonet in 1860. The resemblance was especially strong in Mies's arm chair version of the MR Chair. However, Mies incorporated a new material, a new technology in the use of the cantilever principle, and a much more simplified and straightforward form.

The MR Chair's simplified form resulted from its innovative framework and upholstery. The frame of the side chair consisted of three separate pieces of 24-mm (^{15}⁄₁₆″) nickel-plated tubular steel, bent to form the frame for the back, seat, and semicircular sled base and joined by dowels and screws or welding. Two additional curved rods, which wrapped around the back, screwed to the sides of the top of the frame, and clipped to the lower legs with metal bands, formed the arms of the arm chair. Onto the tubular frame was then attached one of three coverings: leather, canvas, or caning. When leather slings composed the seat and back, the seat of both the side chair and the arm chair was wrapped around the frame and secured with leather ties. The back sling, however, was secured differently on the side

FIGURE 10
The MR Chair

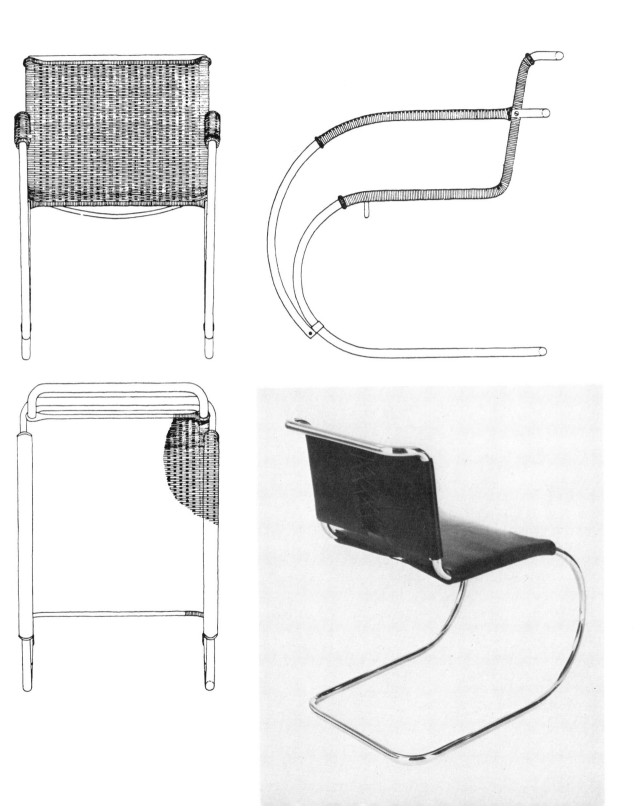

chair than on the arm chair. In the side chair version, it was merely screwed in place, whereas in the arm chair it was secured with ties like the seat. When canvas was used, it was wrapped around the frames and stitched in place. The third covering which was natural or black lacquer caning, was woven directly on the frame to form a continuous seat and back.

The side chair measured 470 mm (18½") wide, 720 mm (28⁵⁄₁₆") deep, and 790 mm (31") high, with a 440-mm (17⁵⁄₁₆") seat height. The arm chair measured 520 mm (20⁷⁄₁₆") wide, 820 mm (32¼") deep, and 790 mm (31") high, with a seat height of 440 mm (17⁵⁄₁₆").

Variations in the chair have occurred in both the frame and the upholstery technique. The nickel plating of the original frame was soon replaced with the brighter and shinier chrome plating. Then in the 1964 American production model, polished stainless steel replaced this chrome plating. As for the covering, neither canvas nor black caning is now available. The leather back sling like the original seat sling, now attaches with ties in both the arm and the side chairs, but the ties are made of nylon. The current production model of the original MR Chair has changed in size as well. The side chair now measures 495 mm (19½") wide, 690 mm (27¼") deep, and 790 mm (31") high, with a seat height of 445 mm (17½"). The arm chair measures 535 mm (21") wide, 825 mm (32½") deep, and 790 mm (31") high, with a seat height of 445 mm (17½") and an arm height of 650 mm (25⁵⁄₈").

Mies designed a lounge version of the MR Chair in 1931. Manufactured first by Bamberg Metallwerkstätten in Berlin and later by

Gebrüder Thonet, this version had a deeper frame and a seat angled slightly lower for greater comfort in relaxed seating. The original upholsteries were available on this frame. In 1977, Knoll reintroduced a padded version of the upholstery that was quilted in nine rows and rested on leather or rubber straps. The lounge adapted the original sophisticated and distinguished lines of the MR Chair.

Barcelona Chair

An epitome of the Contemporary classic, the Barcelona Chair was designed by Mies van der Rohe in 1929 to complement the German Pavilion at the International Exhibition in Barcelona, Spain. Like the building housing it, the chair was stately and elegant.

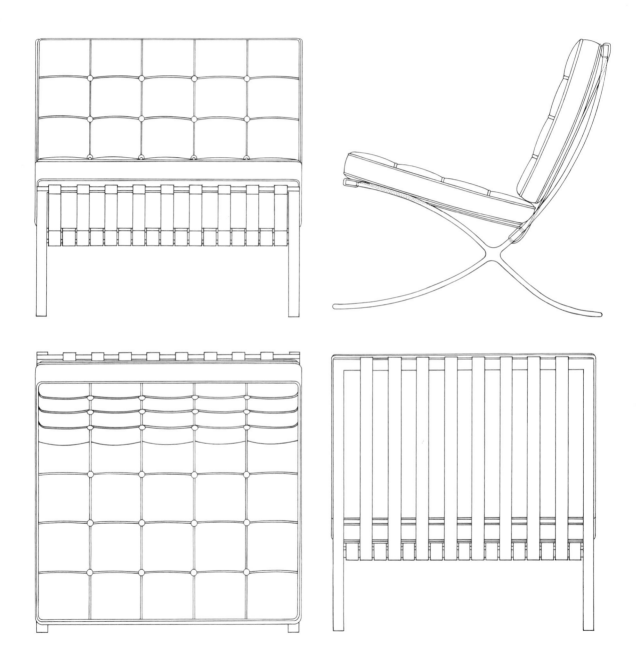

FIGURE 11
The Barcelona Chair

While he was working in Barcelona on a German industrial exhibit, the German government asked Mies to design a national pavilion. This last-minute request came after France and England decided to erect national pavilions. The building would be used first for the inaugural ceremonial signing by King Alfonso VIII of Spain, which would open the German sector of the exhibition, and later as the site of many receptions. The pavilion Mies designed consisted of a small hovering space which, because of an almost unlimited budget, utilized a wide range of elegant and expensive materials: onyx, green Tinian marble, Roman travertine, gray and green transparent glass, and chrome-plated steel. Mies was able to find only one suitable block of onyx because he was searching in the winter, when onyx could not be quarried. Mies therefore made the pavilion twice the block's height, and based all other proportions on it. The richness of materials provided the only decoration of the space or of its furnishings. Though the Barcelona Pavilion stood for less than a year, it was later acclaimed as a milestone in Modern architecture.

The most renowned piece of furniture in the pavilion was the Barcelona Chair. Its visual lightness, simplicity, quality of materials and crafting accorded with the open, flowing character of the architectural setting.

The Barcelona Chair consisted of two rectangular cushions supported by leather straps which were attached to a steel frame. The X-shaped frame became its trademark: An arc which flowed downward supported the back cushion and formed the front legs; the back leg and seat support formed a *cyma recta* curve.

The overall dimensions of the chair were: 762 mm (30") wide, 762 mm (30") deep, and 762 mm (30") high, with a seat height of 430 mm (17").

The face of the original cushions consisted of one rectangular piece of pigskin which was buttoned and tufted. This feature was reworked for the Tugendhat residence the following year, when twenty pieces of leather were sewn together with welting and biscuit-tufting. The stuffing, originally specified to be traditional cotton, horsehair, and burlap, was later changed to more durable foam rubber. Initially, chrome-plated flat-bar steel was used, although in the United States production, it has been replaced with the more durable polished stainless steel. The steel sections of the frame were welded to form flawless connections best exemplified by the intersection of the leg. This joinery, the hand-polished finish, and the detailed, exacting work in leather accounted for the high cost of production.

Lilly Reich, Mies's coworker and confidante, is now credited with assisting in the design of the cushions—the choice of leather, the use of buttons and tufting, and the later padding. But this claim does not discount the meticulous proportioning, detailing, or basic designing accomplished by Mies himself.

The impact of the Barcelona Chair on Contemporary design proved phenomenal. Succeeding attempts to imitate the integrity and craftsmanship of the piece have repeatedly failed. For more than half a century, it has provided the elegance that it so beautifully contributed to its original setting in Barcelona.

Barcelona Ottoman

Mies van der Rohe's Pavilion of 1929 contributed another outstanding statement of contemporary furniture: the Barcelona Ottoman, companion

FIGURE 12

The Barcelona Ottoman

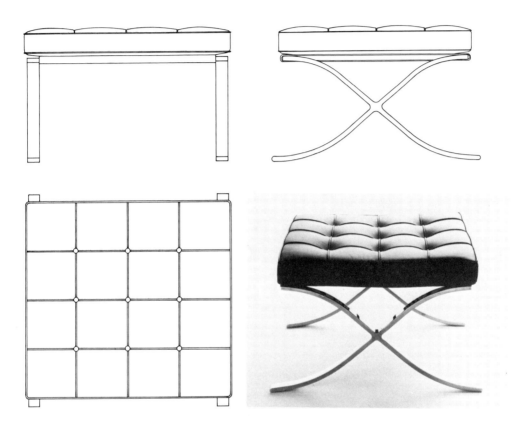

to the Barcelona Chair (Figure 11). Although less frequently discussed and therefore possibly less widely known than the Barcelona Chair, the Barcelona Ottoman was a no less dynamic design.

The pavilion was designed to be a ceremonial setting, and only two Barcelona Chairs were specified, to emphasize the fact that a king and his queen would be present. For additional seating, seven Barcelona Ottomans were strategically placed to complement these two chairs, enhancing the royal environment.

Throughout history, from the Egyptians to the Neoclassics, X-shaped legs have been used for small, low stools. But Mies gave a new grace to this traditional leg through elegant and inviting proportions. The overall dimensions of Mies's Barcelona Ottoman are: 585 mm (23") wide, 560 mm (22") deep, and 370 mm (14½") high, with a seat height of 370 mm (14½").

The shape of the X-base varies slightly from the Barcelona Chair base. In the Barcelona Chair the "X" was formed by a single curved arc and the *cyma recta* cross-member. In the

Barcelona Ottoman two of these *cyma recta* curves are crossed to form the base. Otherwise the basic construction and concept of the two pieces of furniture are the same. The seat of the Ottoman, a cushion of sixteen individually sewn, welted, biscuit-tufted, and buttoned pieces of leather, is supported by seven leather straps that are screwed into the transversal bars of the frame.

Like most pieces of furniture with a more than fifty-year history, the Barcelona Ottoman has undergone several changes and adaptations since its debut in 1929. The first change occurred in 1930, when the Ottoman was once again used by Mies in the Tugendhat residence in Brno. Photographs of the living room of the house show a more defined upholstery due to the introduction of welting. Subsequent versions retained this feature. As on most steel furniture from this period, chrome plating replaced the original nickel plating. Today, the frames of the U.S. models of the ottoman and the chair are made of polished stainless steel. When Knoll began to manufacture the ottoman in 1948, under Mies's supervision a sling-seat version was added. In 1962 Mies designed yet another adaptation: a custom bench, extended in length with four X-legs. Examples of this piece can be found in the New National Gallery in Berlin.

Tables were inspired as well. For the pavilion, two large glass top tables used the basic X-form for their support. Later, for his own Chicago apartment, Mies created a table by removing the cushion of an ottoman and using the base as the support for a travertine top.

Throughout the years, the Barcelona Ottoman has served its purpose well. It has quietly complemented Mies's other furniture while beautifully standing alone.

Tugendhat Chair

Striving for the ultimate in comfort by means of the cantilever principle, Mies van der Rohe designed the Tugendhat Chair in 1930 to enhance the interiors of the celebrated Tugendhat Residence in Brno, Czechoslovakia. This new design synthesized the affluence of the Barcelona Chair (Figure 11) with the resiliency of the cantilevered MR Chair (Figure 10).

The Barcelona Pavilion of 1929 inspired the conception of the Tugendhat house. Mr. and Mrs. Tugendhat commissioned Mies to design their residence after Mrs. Tugendhat visited the pavilion. Being more interested in the Modern movement than her husband was, she persuaded him to accept the dynamic design that Mies proposed. The plan of the house was similar to the pavilion's, though specific requirements of the family necessitated more privacy. Again, Mies used lavish materials: onyx, wood, and glass for walls; chrome-plated columns; natural wool rugs; silk draperies; and glass and chrome tables. Collaborating with Lilly Reich, Mies used rich wood veneers, at times combined with chrome, in much of the custom cabinetry. Like the pavilion, the Tugendhat Residence is remembered today for its spatial relationships, its contrasting yet complementary materials, and its sensitivity to details.

The Tugendhat Chair, named after its clients, was a functional, comfortable composition consisting of upholstered cushions resting on a

FIGURE 13
The Tugendhat Chair

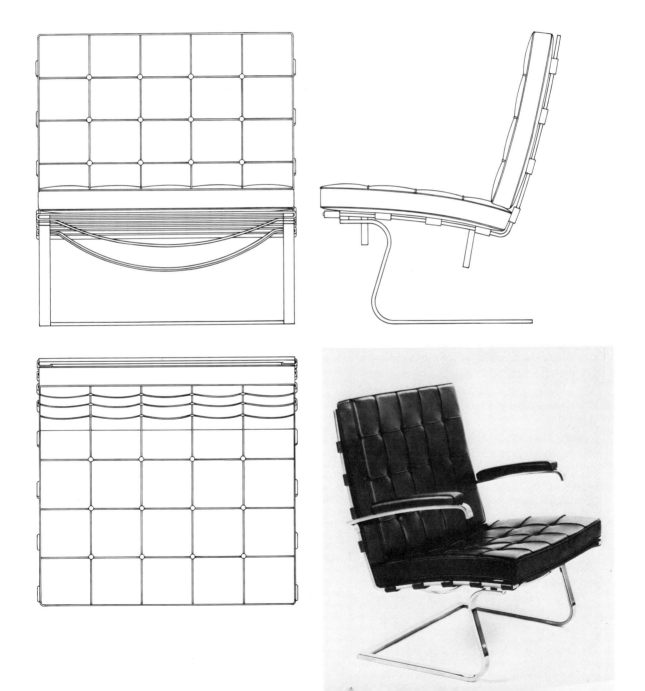

cantilevered steel framework. Eight buckled leather straps encircled the sides of the frame and provided support for the seat and back cushions. Upholstery was available in leather or plain fabric, with or without buttons and tufting. The symmetrical arc of the earlier MR Chair was replaced by an inverted S-shape to form the cantilever support. Mies included arms in the design in order to add to its overall appearance as well as to provide a convenient means of support for leaving the chair. The cushion frame, horizontal braces, arms, and cantilevered sled base were constructed in chrome-plated bar steel. All connections were welded with the exception of the arms and the cantilevered base; which were screwed into place.

Like the Barcelona Chair, the Tugendhat Chair of today differs from the original in that it makes use of polished stainless steel instead of chrome-plated steel. The overall dimensions of the original chair have also changed. The original measured 875 mm (34¾") high, 770 mm (30¼") wide, and 700 mm (27⅝") deep. The model produced today has a height of 815 mm (32").

Mies designed several variations on the theme of the Tugendhat Chair. The first of these changes, for example, called for tubular steel for the frame in lieu of flat bar steel. This variation was first shown in the Berlin Building Exhibition of 1931. By 1936, Mies had applied for a patent on at least twelve interpretations of the Tugendhat form, each with a different shape for the base and arms. None, however, became as popular as the original.

Although the Tugendhat Chair never enjoyed the prestige and acceptance of the Barcelona Chair or the popularity of the MR Chair, it marked a further development of Mies's work in steel furniture. It amalgamated the characteristics of these earlier designs and succeeded in surpassing both in comfort.

Brno Chair

The Brno Chair, named after the Czechoslovakian city in which the Tugendhats lived, fulfilled the family's need for a compact dining chair. Plans called for an extension table to seat twenty-four persons, and use of the earlier MR Chair (Figure 10) proved awkward because its arms extended too far beyond the seat. Consequently, Mies created the Brno Chair, a resilient cantilevered design with a shallow, compact supporting curve. For dining, this chair proved to be more functionally suitable.

Like many of Mies's designs, the Brno Chair was executed in both tubular steel and flat bar steel. (The majority of the pieces in the residence were of tubular steel; only one, a desk chair in Mrs. Tugendhat's bedroom, was of today's more common flat bar steel.) The different natures of these two materials resulted in slight variations in the two versions' structural design. In the tubular steel version two tubes were welded or screwed to form a continuous frame that supported the seat and back and formed the arms and cantilever support. In the flat bar version, the frame terminated in a connection at the sides of the chair back and in the sled base, and a brace was required to stabilize the sides of the cantilever support. These three sections were welded together.

FIGURE 14

**The Brno Chair
(flat bar version)**

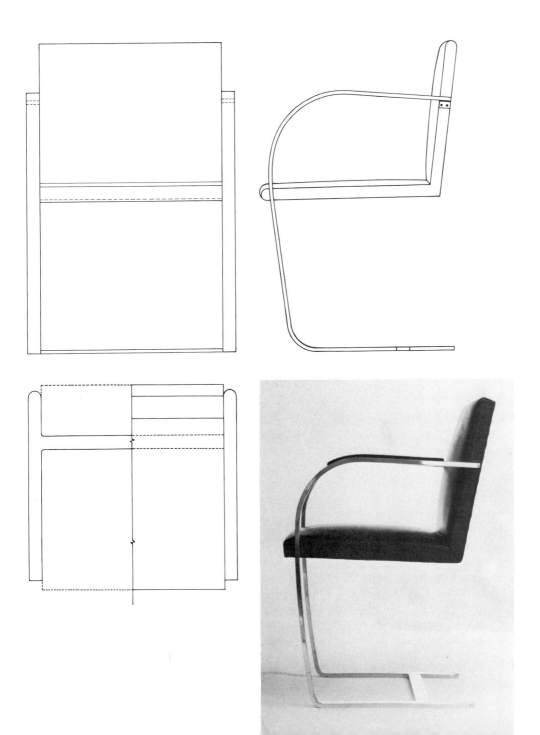

The two versions of the chair had many similarities. Their seat and back constructions were identical, although the wooden seat and back frames were connected with metal studs to the tubular steel frame. The original Brno Chairs were upholstered in leather, including arm covers, though plain fabric was also available. Lacquer, nickel, or chrome-plated finishes on the frames were available; the Tugendhat examples were chrome-plated.

The two versions of the chair did not have identical dimensions; the tubular steel version varied slightly from the flat bar version in width and depth. The original tubular steel version measured 550 mm (21⅝") wide, 730 mm (28⅜") deep, and 786 mm (30⅞") high, while the original flat bar version measured 410 mm (16⅛") wide and 570 mm (22⅜") deep.

Both the 35-mm (1⅜") wide, 11-mm (⁷⁄₁₆") thick flat bar version and the 24-mm (¹⁵⁄₁₆") tubular steel versions are still in production today. Philip Johnson (1906–) popularized the flat bar version in America when he specified it for the Four Seasons Restaurant in the 1958 Seagram Building, a project on which Johnson and Mies collaborated.

Two years later the chair was introduced into mass production. In 1977, the tubular version was reintroduced. The current model of the flat bar steel version measures 585 mm (23") wide, 585 mm (23") deep, and 790 mm (31") high, with a seat height of 445 mm (17½") and an arm height of 655 mm (25¾"). The current model of the tubular steel version measures 560 mm (22") wide, 590 mm (23¼") deep, and 825 mm (32½") high, with a seat height of 440 mm (17¼") and an arm height of 695 mm (27¼").

As he did with the Tugendhat Chair (Figure 13) Mies reviewed and reinterpreted his earlier application of modern materials and construction techniques to produce the Brno Chair. And, though satisfying a client's particular need for dining in 1930, Mies's efforts resulted in a functionally aesthetic chair which is today accepted as a comprehensive statement of his design philosophy.

Tugendhat Table

Mies van der Rohe designed the Tugendhat Table in 1930 to accompany the seating he specified for the Tugendhat residence. Of all his furniture, the table best displayed an integral aspect of his design philosophy—detailed simplicity.

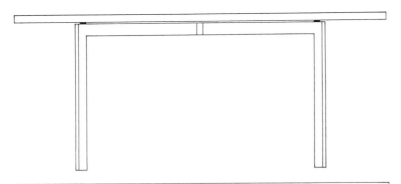

FIGURE 16
The Tugendhat Table

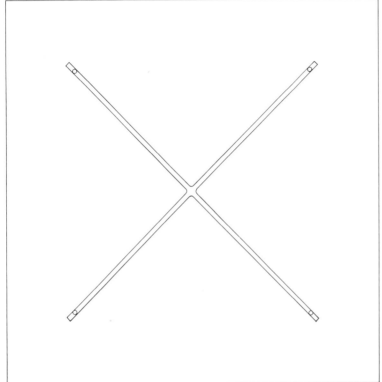

The Tungendhat Table consisted of a four-legged chrome-plated flat bar steel base crowned with a glass top. Visible at the center of the glass, at the top of the X-shaped brace of the four legs, was Mies's famous welded joint. The perfection of its crafting was the only enhancement of the design, besides the natural beauty of the table's materials.

The Tugendhat Table was not the first chrome and glass table that Mies designed. In 1927 he had designed a tubular steel and glass table for the Weissenhof Exhibition. Though also relatively simple, this table was still more complicated than the Tugendhat in its form. Its base consisted of four 24-mm ($^{15}/_{16}$") steel tubes that were welded together to form an "X" which rested on the floor. Four flat bar braces connected the tops of these legs and supported a round black or clear glass top. (This table was reintroduced by Knoll in 1977.) Another glass and chrome table was shown in the Barcelona Pavilion. It had a rectangular black glass top which rested on a pair of X-shaped legs similar to those of the Barcelona Ottoman (Figure 12). In actuality, this was the "Barcelona Table," though today this label is inaccurately used for the 1930 Tugendhat Table.

The source of this misnomer can be easily traced. The current U.S. production model was called the "Barcelona Table" because it beautifully complemented the Barcelona Furniture and was reintroduced into production with that furniture at the same time in 1948. The table was once even known as the "Dessau Table" because Mies, as director of the Bauhaus, was living in Dessau when the table was designed. The most proper name, however, is the one that reflects the piece's place in furniture history, remains the Tugendhat Table.

The dimensions of the table were 550 mm (21⅝") high and 1,000 mm (39⁵/₁₆") square. However, when U.S. production of the table began, variations occurred in the dimensions due to the changeover from millimeters to inches. Today's model measures 430 mm (17") high and 1,015 mm (40") square.

Other variations included the change from nickel or lacquer plating to chrome plating and, in the current U.S. production model, to stainless steel. The originally available black glass and rosewood tops have been discontinued. Today's clear glass top rests on four small rubber tips.

Mies did many studies before arriving at the final design for the Tugendhat Table: he tried round tops, curved legs, three- and five-legged versions, splayed leg versions, and pedestals. Hundreds of takeoffs occurred after the table's introduction, although none captured the sophisticated simplicity of the original Tugendhat Table.

Mies Couch

In 1930 Mies van der Rohe designed a couch that he first used in the New York City apartment of the architect Philip Johnson that same year. The Mies Couch was first publicly shown in Berlin in 1931, in a model bachelor's apartment which Mies designed for the Berlin Building Exhibition. The couch was the first piece of Mies seating furniture that made use of both wood and metal.

This combination of materials along with tufting and welting of the upholstery again evidenced the influence of Mies's associate, Lilly Reich. Mies's association with Reich had developed over a number of years. After both being involved with the German *Werkbund,* they began their professional association in 1927 when they collaborated on the silk exhibition for the *Exhibition de la Mode* in Berlin. Later, they again worked together when Mies designed the 1929 Barcelona Pavilion in Spain. Reich's influence was found in the tufted and buttoned leather cushions of the Barcelona furniture. By 1930, at the Tugendhat residence, the tufting of the furniture was more pronounced, and rich wood veneers were introduced throughout the residence, often in conjunction with steel. Reich had earlier used wood and steel together in her own furniture. Mies used Reich's upholstery technique and the combination of wood and steel in his interpretation of the traditional lounge form.

Like the 1929 Barcelona furniture, the Mies Couch was a reworking of a traditional piece of furniture. Couches had been an essential item of furniture in affluent life-styles during the Egyptian, Greek, and Roman periods of history. These ancient couches usually were composed of rectangular frames on legs, with padding over a slatted or corded support. Again popular in eighteenth- and nineteenth-century Europe, the couch was made more complicated with the introduction of attached upholstery, ornate head and back rests, and sometimes foot rests. Mies, however, returned to the simple, ancient format.

The Mies Couch consisted of a mattress with bolster resting on a wooden frame supported by four tubular steel legs. The foam mattress was upholstered with forty-eight individual pieces of leather sewn together, welted, biscuit-tufted, and buttoned. The 970-mm (38") by 200-mm (8") bolster was secured to the couch frame with a detachable leather strap. The mattress rested on a crisscross webbing of rubber straps. The legs screwed into place and thus made transportation of the couch easier.

Today's model of the Mies Couch remains virtually unchanged, except for a few minor alterations and modifications. The wood frame is smaller, measuring 50 mm (1¹⁵⁄₁₆") thick and 100 mm (3⅞") wide. The straps are now saddle leather over rubber, and they no longer criss-cross the couch but run from side to side. Polyester fiber padding has been added to the mattress, making it firmer and more durable. Also, as on all of Mies's tufted furniture, the tufting, welting, and buttoning on the couch have become more defined. The tubular steel legs are now of polished stainless steel instead of the original chrome-plated steel.

The couch measures 2,000 mm (78⅝") long, 1,000 mm (39⁵⁄₁₆") wide, and 395 mm (15½") high.

The large scale of the couch is not the only Miesian trait. Its exacting details and craftsmanship and its combination of wood, leather, and steel resulted in a formal elegance that is consistent with Mies's design principles.

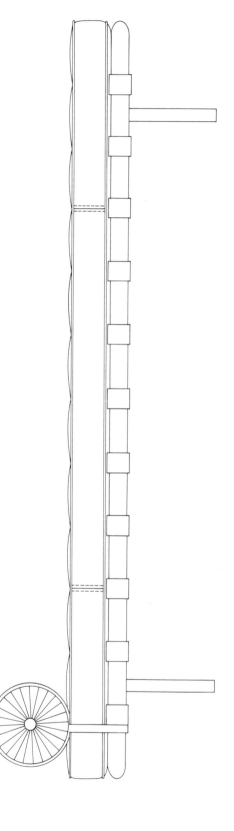

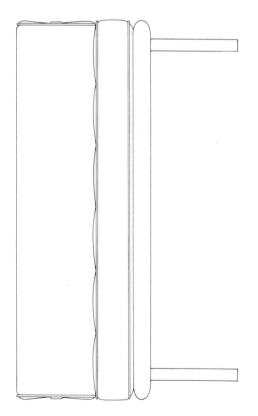

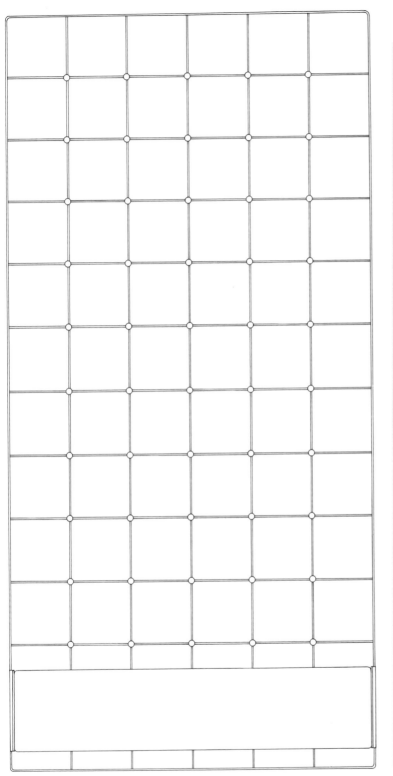

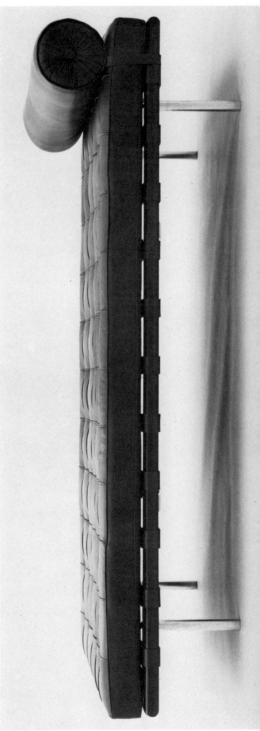

FIGURE 17
The Mies Couch

4

Le Corbusier

Le Corbusier

Contemporary humanity owes a debt of gratitude for Le Corbusier's life of creativity. He was a man of Renaissance dexterity, the epitome of the dynamic architect. He declined to drift with popular architectural currents of his day, but instead forged ahead, leading in two surges of Modern architecture: the Rational Purism of the 1920s and the broader Organic architecture which followed. So inspirational was he that students came from around the world to work without pay in his office. As a city planner in the early 1920s Le Corbusier proposed solutions to many complex urban problems facing city planners today. As an artist he was recognized as a painter, sculptor, and designer of tapestries. A prolific writer, Le Corbusier promoted his theories of modern design in over fifty books and countless articles. And equally important, Le Corbusier was a determined yet sensitive furniture designer. With his colleagues Charlotte Perriand and Pierre Jeanneret (a cousin), he designed standard equipment for modern life-styles, furniture for his architecture— his "machines for living in."

Though frequently denounced by critics and clients for creating cold, inhuman interiors and furnishings, Le Corbusier adhered to his conviction that his design aided twentieth-century life-styles. He believed that a cluttered environment distracted its inhabitants and proved unsanitary. So he purposely reduced the traditional furnishings of interiors but compensated by providing versatile furniture. His "equipment" consisted of well-designed "tools" based on a human scale and universally applicable to all situations.

Le Corbusier was born Charles Edouard Jeanneret-Gris on October 6, 1887, in the famous Swiss watchmaking city of La Chaux-de-Fonds. His family's history in this region dated back to the fourteenth century, when the Albigensians were forcibly expelled from France. Their defiant attitude was later found in Le Corbusier's grandparents: one died in prison, another was involved in the Swiss religiopolitical revolution of 1847. Le Corbusier exulted in the rebelliousness of his ancestors. He also admired his parents. His mother instilled in him the dictum "Whatever you do, see that you do it." His father, an avid hiker, taught him to observe nature by taking him on weekend excursions.

Formal education for Le Corbusier began early. At the age of 4, he entered primary school. By 1900, at the age of 13, he had completed secondary school, and enjoyed the reputation of being a conscientious, talented student. Le Corbusier then enrolled in the Ecole d'Art of La Chaux-de-Fonds to pursue his father's occupation as a watch engraver. He progressed well in his studies, receiving a diploma of honor in 1902 for a watch case that incorporated geometrical and naturalistic forms. (Le Corbusier always wore a watch that he himself had engraved.) But, in spite of this display of engraving talent, one of Le Corbusier's teachers, Charles L'Eplatenier, directed his student toward architecture.

L'Eplatenier introduced Le Corbusier to the masters of classical art, taught him to observe life and to capture what he saw in sketches and drawings, and exposed him to the naturalistic and mathematical aspects of the classical philosophies of Plato and Pythagoras. These influences directly affected Le Corbusier's later work. In 1905, L'Eplatenier initiated Le Corbusier's architectural career by awarding him the commission to design his own residence: Villa Fallet, La Chaux-de-Fonds.

Le Corbusier invested the money from this first commission in travel. He familiarized himself with historical sites of past eras and studied the leading designers of the Modern movement, recording his travels in sketch books. In 1906 he ventured to Italy, where the proportions of Palladio fascinated him. A year later, in Vienna, Le Corbusier came in contact with Josef Hoffmann (1870–1956) and observed the architecture of Adolf Loos (1870–1933).

Though Le Corbusier still called La Chaux-de-Fonds home, he continued to investigate the

beginnings of modern architecture throughout Europe. For two years, from 1908 to 1910, he worked as a draftsman for the Frenchman August Perret in Paris. Then, at the request of his former school, Le Corbusier went to Germany to research industrial design. In Berlin he worked for five months with the leading architect and industrial designer of that era, Peter Behrens, and his employees Walter Gropius and Ludwig Mies van der Rohe. On a visit in 1911 to the Balkans, Asia Minor, and Greece, Le Corbusier was impressed by the whitewashing of the Mediterranean buildings, the geometrical forms of the mosques, and the perfection of the Parthenon. Returning to La Chaux-de-Fonds, he joined his former teacher L'Eplatenier to teach in a new department of the school devoted to architecture and industrial design and continued to practice his own architecture. Through Petrus Berlage's critique of the 1910 Berlin Exhibition, Le Corbusier was introduced to the work of the master architect Frank Lloyd Wright. In 1915 he visited the French architect Tony Garnier, whose work in reinforced concrete had a definite influence on his later work. Finally, in 1916, ten years after beginning his travels and with seven regional architectural commissions behind him, he resolved to leave La Chaux-de-Fonds, which had stifled his dawning architectural concepts, for Paris, the city where creative forces rallied.

In Paris, at 20 rue Jacob in the Saint Germain des Prés district, Le Corbusier rented a small apartment on the seventh floor of a Louis XIV Mansart building, where he lived for seventeen years. His varied interests divided his time. Mornings Le Corbusier devoted to painting. Architecture, which he found much easier, occupied his afternoons. He continued his experimentation in concrete, which dated from his contact with Perret and Garnier. With his design theories in focus, Le Corbusier launched his mature architectural career.

The first public acclamation of Le Corbusier's Contemporary design philosophy resulted from his involvement in the periodical *L'Esprit Nouveau*, which he published with the painter Amédée Ozenfant. Like Ozenfant, Le Corbusier frequently wrote articles for the magazine under a pseudonym. The magazine thus became the source for his professional alias—Le Corbusier, the family name of his maternal grandmother. From 1920 until 1925, the twenty-eight editions of the magazine provided Le Corbusier with a forum for proclaiming his new and controversial ideas on modern design.

Le Corbusier's reassessment of design resulted from his sifting of earlier influences, which he either totally rejected or assimilated. Rejected were the regional and status-conscious traditional designs of his youth. He disregarded design solutions prevalent at the time—de Stijl, the Expressionists, the Constructivists, and the Surrealists—because he found them inappropriate. Le Corbusier rejected Behrens's fanatical utilitarian attitude toward design because he believed it lacked artistic sensitivity, but agreed with Behrens that function and economy through mass production were viable. Influences incorporated into Le Corbusier's concept of design were Wright's open-planning; the international styling of Loos and Hoffmann; the application of contemporary materials of Perret's architecture; the farsighted planning and construction techniques of Garnier; and in particular the purity of form, geometric basis, and sensitivity to proportion of classical buildings such as the Parthenon. Le Corbusier applied these elements, plus his own personal anthropocentric concern, to all areas of his creative genius, and especially to his furniture.

Until the late 1920s Le Corbusier utilized in his interiors the mass-produced furniture available to him, such as the Thonet designs, or relied on current designs by other architects, as in his 1927 Weissenhof interiors furnished by Alfred Roth. While preparing for this exhibition in 1926, Le Corbusier had participated in conversations on the subject of furniture with other young architects being featured, in particular Mies and Stam, who were designing tubular steel furniture that would complement Modern architecture. Later in 1927, Charlotte Perriand, an interior and furniture designer, joined Le Corbusier and his cousin Pierre Jeanneret at the 35 rue de Sèvres studio which was the permanent location of his office throughout his professional life. The collaboration resulted in the most renowned furniture bearing Le Corbusier's name. The Chaise Longue (Figure 18), the *Basculant* Arm Chair (Figure 21), the *Grand Confort Petit* (Figure 20), the *Grand Confort Grand* (Figure 19), and the *Table en Tube d'avion section ovoide* (Figure 22) were first used in Le Corbusier's 1928–1929 Villa Church, Ville d'Avary, Paris, and publicly shown the same year in the Salon d'Automne. Le Corbusier intended for these pieces to be mass-produced and accessible to the general public. Like his architecture, however, his furniture was at that time only for the elite.

Le Corbusier's architectural theories between the years 1920 and 1929 were incorporated in the Puristic proposed project Citrohan, which was first presented in a 1920 issue of *L'Esprit Nouveau*. In 1923 the La Roche/Jeanneret commission in Paris tested these design principles. Similar commissions filled the remainder of the decade: a multiple housing complex in Pessac, France, 1925; the Villa Stein at Fraches, France, 1927; Villa Church, Ville d'Avary, Paris, 1928–1929; and the exemplary Villa Savoy at Poissy, France, 1928–1930. This villa was a light, hovering structure containing a roof terrace, a smooth facade, a horizontal band of windows (made possible by skeleton framing), and interior spaces as free and unbound as the house on its site. The design embodied Le Corbusier's mature Purist concept of residential architecture.

In the early 1930s, however, with a unique new attitude toward materials and form, Le Corbusier shifted away from his previous stark Purism and machinelike geometry. This change resulted in a variety of Organic and sculptural designs evident in his later architecture: the Swiss dormitory at Cité Universitaire, Paris (1931–1933); *Unité de Habitation,* Marseille (1948–1952), which contained the earliest examples of "Brutalism" and exhibited his "modular" system of designing; the Pilgrimage Chapel *La Notre Dame du Haut,* Ronchamp, France (1947–1954), an Organic design; in India the planning and government buildings for the city of Chandigarh, 1951–1957; the Dominican monastery of La Tourette, Eveux, Lyons, France, 1957–1960; and in the year of his death, the

design for the Heidi Weber House, the center for Le Corbusier in Zurich, Switzerland, 1965–1968.

Le Corbusier was a man of slight frame, very lean in his youth. He had a well-defined oblong face with tight lips, a high forehead, and unparted hair combed straight back. In his early thirties he lost the use of his left eye. A skeptical and self-sufficient character, he befriended few. (His lifelong friend and colleague, Charlotte Perriand, did not form a favorable first impression when seeking a position in his studio in 1927. She was told that they did not embroider cushions in his atelier.) Until the 1940s, he smoked heavily—pipes, cigars, and cigarettes. But, being cussedly determined, when challenged by a friend he abruptly stopped. He was able to comprehend many conversations at once, and frequently responded in a visual way with a comprehensive sketch. "Sketching" sometimes consisted of full-scale drawings, executed on an oversized blackboard in his studio. He worked in an orderly fashion and like his architecture, functioned best in isolation; he reserved a 3-by-3-meter room in his office to do private meditation. In his daily dress he maintained the same sense of standardization and formality seen in his architecture. He wore a fresh white collar, a dark bow tie and hat, and, always, dark-rimmed glasses. Throughout most of his life academia, bureaucracy, and the general public misunderstood and misused Le Corbusier and his architecture. A determined man, he fought with tenacity, and finally achieved acceptance in his later years.

Le Corbusier became a French citizen in

1930 when he married Yvonne Gallis, a former fashion model. They had no children. He died on August 27, 1965, while swimming in the Mediterranean off the coast of Cap Martin near Monte Carlo. On September 1, 1965, France honored him with a state funeral at the Louvre.

Chaise Longue

The Chaise Longue was the most relaxing piece of furniture Le Cobusier designed for residential interiors. Its adjustability allowed a range of choice from virtually upright seating to the feet-above-head position of complete repose.

The influences behind Le Corbusier's Chaise Longue are intriguing. Though many comparisons have been drawn between the upper framework and Thonet's 1860 Rocker (Figure 2), the most direct link is to the lower Thonet Rocker of 1880. (This rocker was reintroduced by Gebrüder Thonet in November 1977 in a limited edition of 200.) In this version the head, back, seat, and foot rest blended to form a continuous surface. Undulating curved braces connected the lounge surface to the rocker's runners. Le Corbusier purified Thonet's design by eliminating its curved bracing and reducing its elements to a lounge surface with an arc runner, decisions which reflected Le Corbusier's dependence on regular geometric forms. In addition, Le Corbusier designed a four-legged base which stabilized the selected lounge position. Without the base, if desired, the lounge could be used as a rocker.

The inspiration for Le Corbusier's selection of durable pony skin, the Chaise Longue's most characteristic upholstery, is also traceable. Being Swiss, he was accustomed to seeing Swiss army troops carrying their rugged backpacks of horsehide. He recognized that this material was appropriate for his lounge because it was durable and provided an aesthetic contrast to the metal. Because of its additional markings, pony skin was Le Corbusier's choice for the upholstery of his lounge.

The makeup of the Chaise Longue demonstrated the Purist concept of separation of supporting and supported elements. The supported tubular steel framework consisted of a lounge surface frame which gave direct support to the human body, mounted on gliding arc runners that were totally detached from the four-legged iron base. Friction between the tubular runners and the rubber-covered crossbars of the base sufficed to hold the upper framework in the selected position. Purism was also seen in the separation of the cushioning elements of the lounge. The upholstery pad rested on spring-held metal webbing and snapped around the upper frame at the head and foot. The bolster was anchored with a strap which buckled around the pad and frame.

Many variations were attempted on the design, materials, and finishes of the original version of the Chaise Longue. In the early 1930s, both Thonet (the first manufacturer of Le Corbusier's furniture) and Charlotte Perriand substituted laminated wood, solid wood, or bamboo for the original metal. Changes in the general proportions and structure of the Chaise Longue resulted from these modifications. Today's Chaise Longue, reintroduced in 1965 by

Le Corbusier

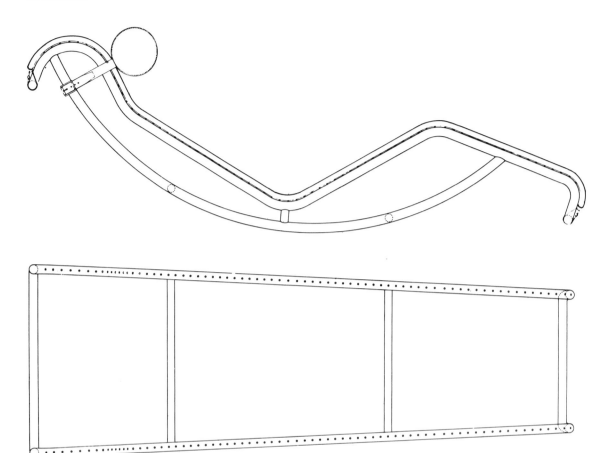

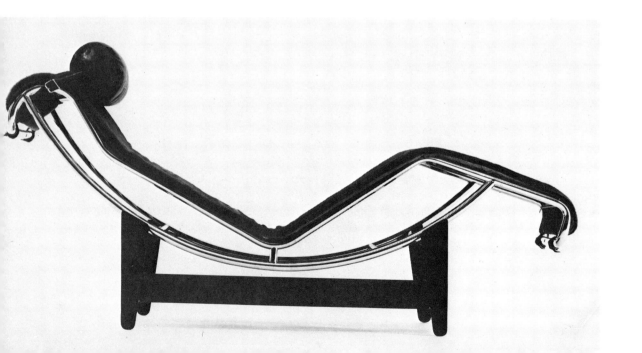

FIGURE 18

The Le Corbusier Chaise Longue

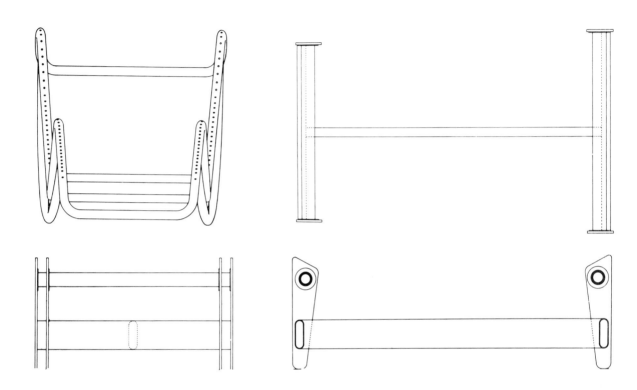

the Milanese manufacturer Cassina, is available with the original chrome or lacquer finish on the tubular steel lounge. However, a black enameled iron base has replaced the original two-toned base of blue-gray stretchers and dark gray legs. Tear-shaped and elliptical cross sections of the stretcher were tried, though today's production has returned to the original oval shape. Protective rubber tips for the feet prevent marring of floor surfaces. The pad, upholstered in pony skin, cow or horsehide, or fabric, rests on a paired wire framework strung on the tubular steel frame. These rubber-coated wires reduce the abrasion on the pad which occurred on the earlier metal webbing. Now as

originally, the bolster is available only in leather and is attached by a leather strap. The dimensions of the Chaise Longue have remained constant: 570 mm (22⅜") wide and 1,600 mm (63") long, with a maximum height of 730 mm (28¾").

At the time of its first public showing in the 1929 *Salon d'Automne*, Le Corbusier presented this explanation of his Chaise Longue in a lecture he gave in Buenos Aires: "We have built it with bicycle frame tubes and we covered it with a magnificent pony skin. . . . I thought of the cowboy from the Wild West, smoking his pipe, his feet in the air higher than his head, against the chimney piece: complete rest."

Grand Confort

Le Corbusier was intent on human well-being. His uncluttered rooms were freed for relaxation and thought. Juxtaposing thick, soft cushions with economical tubular steel, he created a warm, secure, sinfully comfortable nest that he called the Grand Confort.

Like all of Le Corbusier's 1928 furniture, the Grand Confort—his modern interpretation of the traditional French Bergère—was designed in Paris. It satisfied a specific need for a comfortable chair for lengthy conversation and reading. It also revolutionized the traditional Bergère form through the introduction of new materials and new structure. The customary concealed wooden frame, on which layers of padding were placed (and later, in the nineteenth century, in which springs were embedded), was simply reduced and transformed into an exposed exterior metal cage that held several soft and distinctive cushions.

Josef Hoffmann's Kubus Chair, designed in 1910, directly influenced the Grand Confort's form. Le Corbusier contacted Hoffmann during his 1907 travels and later frequently praised the farsighted design theories of this precursor of the Modern movement. The influence of Hoffmann's design can be seen in the comfortable, body-hugging shape of the Petit version, the detachment of both versions from the floor, and their Cubistic form. Hoffmann's chair was designed around a standard cube module, an obvious decorative feature. Le Corbusier, on the other hand, did not use geometry as ornament. His geometrical proportions, based on human scale, were an assurance of human comfort.

FIGURE 19
The Grand Confort Grand

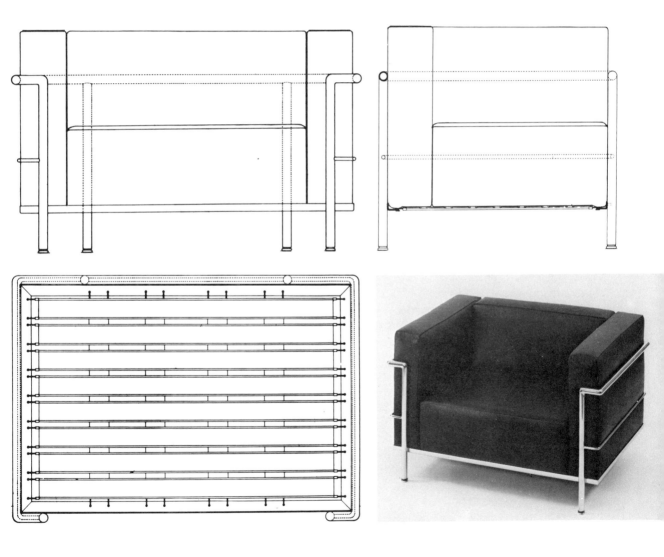

As in traditional French furniture, two versions of the Grand Confort were designed, large and small. They were different not only in width but height and depth as well. The smaller Grand Confort was narrower, but taller and deeper, measuring 760 mm (29⅞") wide, 700 mm (27½") deep, and 670 mm (26⅜") high. The larger version measured 990 mm (39") wide, 680 mm (26¾") deep, and 620 mm (24½") high. The small Grand Confort contained five bulging down-stuffed cushions: two for the seat, two for arms, and one for the back. The larger version had four cushions, providing only one for the seat.

In both versions the exterior steel frame consisted of two shapes of steel: an L-shaped member and two sizes of tubular steel. The L-shaped member, on which springs connected the supporting webbing, formed the foundation for the cushions. The large-diameter tubular steel formed the legs and top railing of the chair's frame, while the smaller tubing braced the legs and contained the cushions. It was bent at the corners and welded to the larger-diameter legs. In contrast, the corners of the upper, larger tube brace were welded (not bent) to form right angles, resulting in a more geometric form.

The original supple down filler has been replaced by a more economical and durable combination of rubberized cocoa fiber, foam polyurethane, and polyester fibers. This lends a crisper look to the chair. Leather or plain fabric is still specified for the upholstery of the cushions.

In the current production, changes have also occurred in the design's finishes. When originally specified at the Villa Church in 1929, the tubular steel segments were lacquered light blue-gray to contrast with the dark leather cushions, while the dark gray L-shaped member blended with them. Today, the metal frame is finished in nickel, chrome, or one of at least six different-colored lacquers.

FIGURE 20
The Grand Confort Petit

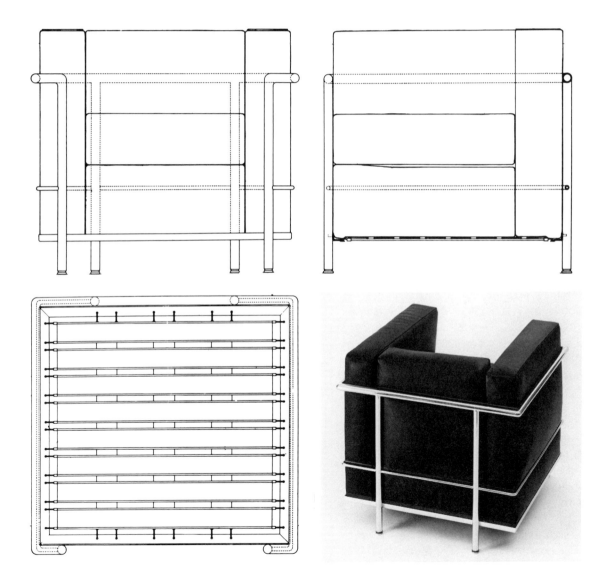

Basculant Chair

Recognizing a need for variety in seating, Le Corbusier rounded off his 1928 collection by designing the Basculant Chair. Its visual as well as actual light weight made it a comfortable chair for active conversation.

With the Basculant, Le Corbusier did not clearly distinguish between the supporting structural frame and the seat and back, as he had with the Chaise Longue (Figure 18) and the Grand Confort (Figures 19 and 20). Instead, these functions were blended. The seat was slung on a brace of the chair's frame which curved upwards. This brace supported the point of attachment of the seat and back frames. On its upper curve, a single pivotal connection with the back allowed the back to conform to the user's posture. The upper curve of this brace also aided the design's stability by providing a raised point of connection to the back legs. The four vertical tubular steel legs with horizontal braces at the front and back formed two H-shapes which were traversed on each side by the seat/back support. Leather, fabric, pony skin, cowhide, or horsehide upholstery formed the seat and back. Springs held the upholstery taut and resilient on the chair's frame. This ingenious composition resulted from and affirmed the technology of its day.

Le Corbusier's selection of furniture materials and construction processes also reflected his fascination with modern technology. The fact that tubular steel, a strong and innovative material, was used in the Basculant Chair made possible its delicate form. Instead of bending this material, as had his contemporaries, Le Corbusier made use of the new technical process of welding. By stipulating that the chair's corners be mitered and welded, he created a more geometric, machinelike form. In some cases Le Corbusier was directly

FIGURE 21
The Basculant Chair

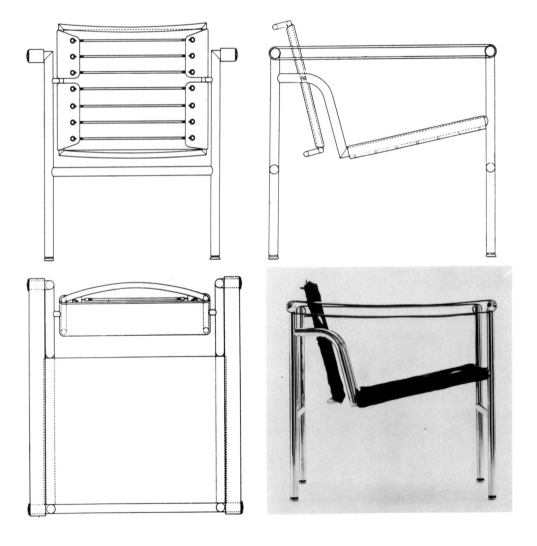

influenced by the look of machinery: The Basculant Chair's arm straps are very similar to machine belting; and the action of the pivotal back emphasized movement, an innate facet of any machine. However, the machine look was not his only design inspiration.

The Basculant Chair also shows the influences of two previous furniture designs: the nineteenth-century Colonial Chair (designer and exact date unknown) and Marcel Breuer's Wassily Chair (Figure 5) of 1925. The Basculant Chair's obvious similarities to the Colonial Chair were its sling upholstery, strap arms, adjustable pivotal back, and economical, linear makeup. The features were undoubtedly admired by Le Corbusier; he later used the Colonial Chair in his own 1938 apartment in rue Nungesser et Coli in Paris. The impact of Breuer's Wassily Chair was evident in the Basculant's use of tubular steel and in its Cubist form. Though a close relationship exists, the Wassily Chair seems complicated and excessive in its size and use of materials when compared to the precision of the Basculant Chair.

The Basculant Chair measured 600 mm (23⅝") wide, 650 mm (25⅝") deep, and 640 mm (25¼") high, with a seat height of 400 mm (15¾").

Photographs of the chair in the Villa Church (1928–1929) showed variations not found in the 1929 *Salon d'Automne* version, which was mass-produced by Gebrüder Thonet, or in succeeding models. For the Villa setting, the chair had a more complex upholstery with padding and welting.

Both of these original versions had arm straps tapering from the front to the back. Today, the strap is straight. An additional brace has been added at the top of the back support to prevent the sides from splaying. Except for this small alteration the frame remains unchanged.

Le Corbusier Table

In 1928 Le Corbusier and his associates designed the furniture "equipment" they considered necessary for the contemporary lifestyle. Their collection included a variety of chairs, a chaise longue, and a table—the *Table tube a'avion* (the table of airplane tubes).

This table, even more than the Grand Confort Chairs (Figures 19 and 20), was Puristic in structure. A rectangular top either of clear and ' gold-tinted plate glass or of wood was supported by a base of metal. Oval tubes were used in the two inverted U-shapes which formed the table's four legs and in their connecting stretcher. Four slender leveling devices screwed into place between the top and the base at the corners exaggerated the distinction between the table's supporting and supported elements and gave the top its distinctive floating characteristic.

All of Le Corbusier's furniture was influenced by modern machinery and Classical geometric proportions. The Table was no exception. Certainly one of the newest machines, and therefore extremely fascinating to Le Corbusier, was the airplane. The Table's use of oval tubes, as well as the welding together of these tubes and even the introduction of the leveling screws to the posts, reflected this fascination. But also important in the development of the Table was Le Corbusier's keen geometric sensitivity in arriving at its dimensions: 850 mm (33½") wide, 2,250 mm (90") long, and 690 mm (27⅛") high. The glass was 18 mm (⅝") thick and the wooden top was 36 mm (1⅜") thick.

The Table, along with Le Corbusier's other furniture, is still manufactured today. The present production model varies slightly from the original. The gold-tinted glass top that was originally shown is no longer available; only clear glass or wooden tops can be specified. Metal posts have replaced the leveling devices on which the top originally rested. The tubes continue to be oval and have recently been made available in Le Corbusier's color palette of at least six different lacquer selections.

Le Corbusier's name for this table—*Table tube d'avion*—blatantly advertised the new technology involved with its production. Like the Villa Savoy, which appeared in the same year, the top of the Table balanced on slender supports. Le Corbusier's fascination with this Puristic detail continued and was later displayed in one of his most Organic structures, the Ronchamp Chapel, whose bulky roof was precariously supported atop minute posts. This floating feature of the chapel, both in scale and effect, undoubtedly stemmed from the design of the *Table tube d'avion*.

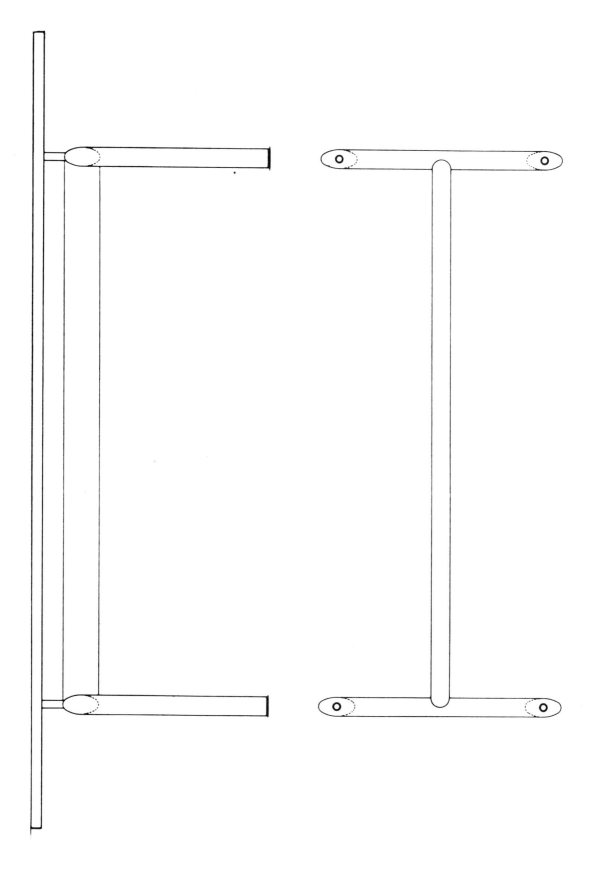

FIGURE 22

The Le Corbusier Table

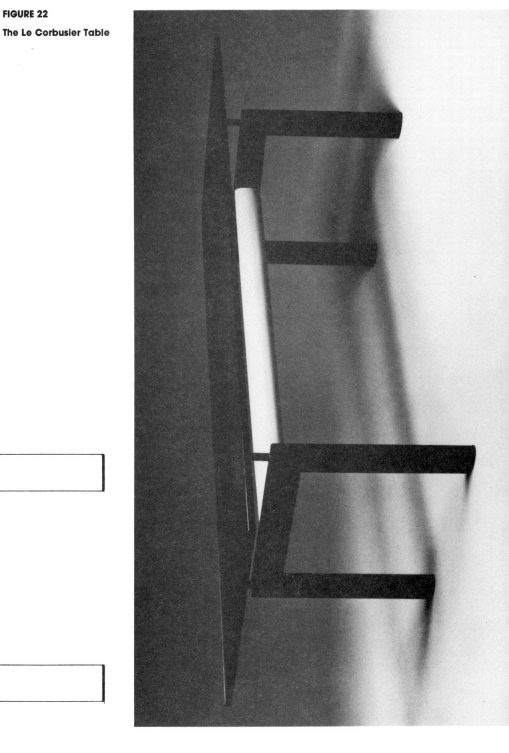

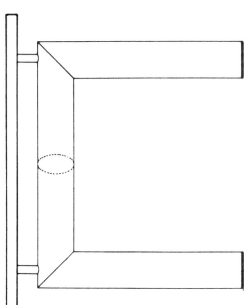

Scandinavian Design:
The Nordic Option

After what was considered by many to be a rather austere beginning, the newly established Contemporary movement soon began to diversify. Though the new materials and forms of the late 1920s captivated much of the design world in Europe and America, they did not satisfy everyone. No matter how practical and pure the beauty of chromed steel, there were those among the population, particularly in regions with harsher climates, who would never consider Le Corbusier's Chaise Longue the answer to their personal dream of complete repose. Multiformity was needed to meet the furnishing needs of the modern consumer market more completely.

Scandinavian designers provided the first alternatives. Instead of metal, they made use of wood in every conceivable form, both new and old. Although they pioneered dynamic techniques of construction, they placed less emphasis on the machine look and machine crafting. When readily available, hand-crafting was proudly employed as a sensible and valid means of twentieth-century expression. From the outset, the concern of Scandinavian designers was not bringing the machine in—their countries were far from being fully industrialized—but bringing quality back.

Each of the major Scandinavian exporters—Sweden, Finland, Denmark—had its design distinctions and period of primary influence. Sweden made the first international impact in the early 1930s. Desire to capture foreign markets led designers such as Bruno Mathsson to produce lightweight, quickly assembled designs keyed for economical shipment. By the close of the decade, the pacesetting forms and construction techniques of the Finn Alvar Aalto had been successfully introduced to both America and Europe. Due to the international trend back to natural materials, the Dane's sophisticated solid wood designs, as well as all Scandinavian products in general, enjoyed a boom period after World War II. Hans J. Wegner, Finn Julh, Børge Mogenson, and Jens Risom (who later worked in the United States) were worldwide successes.

The outstanding designs of Aalto and Wegner not only provided optimum proof of the sound construction and superb design ability of their movement, they also were prime illustrations of the distant poles of Scandinavian design. Aalto's products, based on technical research and machine production, contrasted to Wegner's pieces, which were at times traditionally crafted of solid wood. Both, however, expressed modern aesthetics through the warm pleasure of wood—providing a welcome option for millions of mid-century consumers.

5

Alvar Aalto

Alvar Aalto was publicly admired and professionally respected as a productive twentieth-century architect and furniture designer. His work spanned over sixty years. And though Aalto's influence reached far beyond the borders of his homeland, his designs originated as specific solutions to his region's needs.

Finland was Aalto's home. This single fact was the most dominant force in his contribution to design. The young nation's location, isolation, and desire for a new, independent national style created the necessary climate of design freedom, and its natural resources provided the inspiration and means for Aalto's work. From Finland's social traditions and severe climatic conditions Aalto learned a sensitivity to human needs as well as to nature that remains his major gift to an admiring world.

Aalto was born Hugo Alvar Henrik Aalto on February 3, 1898, in Kuortane, a small Finnish township in Ostro-Bothnia. His father was J. H. Aalto, a surveyor; his mother, Selma Hackstedt Aalto, was the daughter of Hugo Hamilkar Hackstedt, a forester and teacher. Together, his father and maternal grandfather enormously influenced Aalto's intellectual development.

They planted a unique attitude from which few modern designers have been able to benefit: intimacy with nature and the habit of approaching one's career as a public servant.

In 1903 Aalto's family moved to Jyväskylä in the central lake district of Finland, where he attended local primary and secondary schools. He left home in 1916 to study architecture at the Helsinki Institute of Technology. Finland declared independence from Russia on December 6, 1917, and Aalto postponed his studies in 1918 to join the White side of the ensuing civil conflict, seeking liberation from both the Russian Czar and the rising Bolshevik regime.

The nonsocialist Finns were victorious in May 1918. Independence presented an intriguing and exciting problem to Finland's architectural community: How would the new national identity be expressed in architecture? The beginnings of Aalto's design career paralleled this historical development.

Until the fall of 1918, Aalto worked and traveled in Finland with other young architects whom he had met during his military service. Then he returned to his formal architectural studies in Helsinki.

As a student under the architect Armas

Lindgren (1874–1929), Aalto investigated the new Classical trend in Scandinavia's architecture which was replacing the National Romanticism of the late nineteenth and early twentieth centuries. After graduating in 1921, Aalto evidenced this growing new trend in his early professional work. After serving his regular tour of military duty from June 1922 until March 1923, the young architect established his first independent office in Jyväskylä.

In October 1924, Aalto married Aino Marsio, a former employee, whom he then made a partner in his architectural office. For their honeymoon they took a plane to northern Italy, quite a novel means of transportation at this time, requiring a stopover in Vienna. This trip substantially added to Aalto's classical knowledge. At the same time, Aalto's enthusiasm for aviation led him to develop a unique viewpoint on the interrelationship between nature and human designs. It also provided him images such as the undulating contours he used later, which were stimulated by aerial views of hundreds of Finnish lakes. When the couple returned they began a productive collaboration in both architecture and furniture design.

Like other young designers of the 1920s, he gradually redirected his style to the Contemporary modes of France and Germany. But because of his Finnish background, Aalto was unable to justify their fanaticism for producing "rational" design. He found it inapplicable to his particular circumstance. By the late 1920s Aalto's architecture still drew from the Modern concepts of others but began to include his own innovations as well.

Aalto's maturing architectural style was emerging when he moved his office to Turku in 1927. By 1929, Aalto had been awarded four major architectural projects, all won through competitions. What distinguished Aalto's designs from those of other Contemporary designers was their orientation to the site and the sun, their well-planned lighting, their acoustics, and their warm materials. In addition, Aalto used undulation to free the static Contemporary form. With these elements Aalto introduced a humane facet to Modern architecture not present before. Aalto was fortunate. His young country recognized his unique talents and had the foresight to entrust its architectural future to a young designer.

During the 1930s Aalto was acknowledged not only in his homeland but also internationally. In 1933 his work was shown in London in an exhibition organized by *The Architectural Review*. The same year he relocated his offices in Helsinki, Finland's capital and largest city, and became a leader in its architectural community. In 1936 he completed his office/home complex in Mukkiniemi just outside Helsinki. He won the competition to design the Finnish Pavilion at the 1937 Paris World's Fair. Again in 1938 he executed the design for the Finnish Pavilion at the 1939 New York World's Fair.

This New York commission opened a decade of shuttling between the United States and Finland. To begin preparation of the fair exhibition space and to lecture at a showing of his work at the Museum of Modern Art (MOMA) in New York, Aalto made his first trip to North America in 1938. The next year he made his second visit, to complete the pavilion's installation and to attend its opening. It was during this 1939 visit to the United States that Aalto met the pioneering Contemporary American architect Frank Lloyd Wright. Wright unreservedly admired and endorsed Aalto's work—an honor few European architects of that time could boast. When soon after his return home, Finland once again found itself at war, Aalto left his successful practice to enlist in the Finnish Ski Patrol. As soon as a peace agreement was reached in March 1940, Aalto returned to America. During this visit he attended the opening of the second season of the World's Fair and accepted a professorship at the Massachusetts Institute of Technology in Cambridge, Massachusetts. He taught at M.I.T. during the fall quarter but left in December for Finland, where he remained for the duration of the Second World War.

Circumstances of this period of conflict initiated a rash of building which afforded Aalto further opportunities to design. During the "Winter War" with Russia, Finland had lost 12 percent of its land, and thousands of Finnish refugees, who refused to live under Russian rule, had to be housed. Damages of World War II compounded Finland's housing problems. In addition to city planning, Aalto was also engaged in designing hospitals and defense structures.

In 1946 Aalto was reinstated as a professor at M.I.T., though he maintained his office in Helsinki. This setup necessitated frequent Atlantic crossings. After the death of his wife Aino in 1949, however, he returned to Finland to practice full-time.

Three years after Aino's death, Aalto married another architect, Elissa Makiniemi, and together they designed until his death on May 11, 1976. (She continues in the practice today.) Well-established by the 1950s, Aalto, unlike many Contemporary masters, never had difficulty maintaining a full work load; in fact, he became Finland's architect laureate. His design related both to his time and to his people; he captured the young nation's spirit.

Though Aalto's architecture could be found around the world, the best of it was located in Finland. Over one span of his career, his designs ranged from hospitals to printing plants to exclusive private residences. Most outstanding were the Viipuri Library in Viipuri, Finland (now Russia) (1927–1935); the Paimio Sanatorium in Paimio, Finland (1928–1933); the Finnish Pavilion at the New York World's Fair (1939); the Villa Mairea in Noormarkku, Finland (1938–1939); the Baker House Dormitory at M.I.T. in Cambridge,

Massachusetts (1947–1949); Finlandia Hall in Helsinki, Finland (1962–1971); and an addition to the Congress Hall in Helsinki, Finland (1974).

Concerned with every facet of his architecture, Aalto began early in his career to design custom furniture for his interiors. He quickly directed his design toward mass production, creating standard parts which could easily be adapted for specific situations. Often individual pieces were personalized with special upholstery or finishes for special clients. Therefore, Aalto's furniture, though mass-produced, did not seem like machine art. It was multifunctional for people of all ages, in both public and private situations.

Aalto's furniture utilized Finland's most abundant natural resource—wood. His recognition of wood's psychological, practical, and economical advantages confirmed it as a major material for twentieth-century furniture design. His innovations proved that wood was as appropriate as tubular steel for use in furniture in our era.

To a Finn, the prospect of returning home after a day of only six hours of daylight and subzero temperatures to lounge in tubular steel furniture was far from inviting. Psychologically as well as physically, the material would have only added to the actual coldness. Aalto's use of wooden furniture provided an alternative. Wood was ideal for his region's needs: it was warmer, quieter, and more natural. When laminated or made into plywood, wood not only was psychologically beneficial, it had a practical advantage over tubular steel as well: It was lighter in weight. It could be easily

curved, stretched, or compressed into a desired shape. Inexpensive joints could be effectively executed. When properly constructed, plywood resisted splitting and warping caused by heat and moisture. It could be made sanitary and was quickly cleanable with Aalto's selection of lacquer finishes. In addition, modern construction techniques such as the cantilever principle could be used.

For Aalto's furniture construction, he selected the native nordic blond birch. This wood was especially suitable: It was flexible, firm-grained, and free of knots—features which Finland had previously exploited in the construction of skis. Since Finland was at that time Europe's major supplier of plywood, Aalto's choice of birch plywood benefited not only him but the national economy as well.

Aalto was by no means the first to recognize the advantages of plied wood. Michael Thonet (1796–1871) and John Henry Belter (1804–1863) had capitalized on plywood's strength and moldability when they utilized it early in the 1800s. Though patents were granted throughout the nineteenth century, plywood's success in general use was hampered because the original glues proved overly sensitive in contact with moisture; this was one of Thonet's reasons for switching to the more durable bentwood. When a suitable adhesive was finally introduced in the late nineteenth century, it led the way for plywood's popularity. By the early twentieth century, plywood could be found in seating for public transportation, in airplane bodies, and as backs and drawer bottoms in furniture. Not until the 1920s was plywood considered again more seriously by furniture designers. When faced with appropriate veneers, it was considered a suitable material for the composition of Art Deco furniture. At the Bauhaus, its functional properties were investigated during the early 1920s by Breuer and many of his classmates.

By 1927, Aalto and his first wife Aino had begun experimenting in molding wood. Their work, however, was not limited to this area alone; they also designed briefly with tubular steel. Their first Modern design was a wooden stacking chair for the auditorium of Aalto's Jyväskylä Civil Guard Building, 1927.

Early in 1929, Aalto began experimenting with molding plywood. With the aid and encouragement of Otto Korhonen, a plywood and furniture producer from Turku, an experimental workshop was established. For the Turku 700 Year Exhibition of 1929, Aalto showed chairs with molded seats and backs. These chairs had both tubular steel and thick laminated cantilevered supports; however, the laminated support was not structurally stable. A variety of furniture, some framed totally of tubular steel and some framed in combination with molded plywood, was shown in the Minimum Apartment in the Helsinki Arts and Crafts Exhibition of 1930. Though it was not shown at this time, Aalto continued to experiment with producing a chair with molded wooden support.

The following year Korhonen started producing Aalto's "Paimio" furniture, his first successful all-plywood designs. With the financial help of Harry and Maire Gullichsen, the international marketing firm of ARTEK was established in Helsinki in 1935. This association of designer, manufacturer, and marketer resulted in a widely accessible collection of furniture that included the Paimio Arm Chair (1929) (Figure 23); the Viipuri Collection (1933–1935) (Figures 24 to 26); the Aalto Serving Cart (1936) (Fig. 27); the Cantilevered Arm Chair (1946) (Fig. 28); and the famous Fan Leg Stool of 1954 (Fig. 29). This furniture continues to be produced by Huonekalutehdas Korhonen and internationally marketed by ARTEK.

Alvar Aalto's design reflected the man's quiet calmness and conviction, as well as his professional confidence in the role he played in molding Finland's design character and in his overall effect as a twentieth-century designer. Although his work was based in the fundamentals of the Modern movement, he broadened the movement's scope. His independence, personal wit and imagination, and sincere concern for "people-design" were revealed in both his furniture and his architecture. Aalto will be remembered and honored as the humanizer of the Machine Age.

Paimio Arm Chair

Alvar Aalto's sensitivity to his clients' welfare was perhaps keenest in the Paimio Tuberculosis Sanatorium commission, which he won through a competition in the fall of 1928. As the architect, interior designer, and furniture designer of the project, Aalto designed the patient and the general services wings of the hospital as well as three staff residential complexes.

The buildings were completed in 1933. In designing them, Aalto went beyond merely providing functional essentials; he created a healthy, cheerful environment in which to live, work, and recuperate. His careful orientation of the wings allowed each patient to awake with sun on the bed. Lounges and dining areas were also positioned to capture the sun. Materials were used which reduced distracting hospital noises; color and lighting were soothing. Routine cleaning and maintenance were efficiently handled with little disturbance to patients and minimum effort from the staff.

This same practical and psychological sensitivity was found in the furniture Aalto designed, particularly in the Paimio Arm Chair. The 110-degree angle of the back was an easement to the TB patient's breathing. The chair was easily moved. The front curve of the arm provided a secure hold for leaving the chair. The surface of the chair was easily cleaned. These features could have been provided in any modern material. But to Aalto the naturalness and familiarity of wood mitigated the coldness of institutional finishing and therefore made it the most appropriate material.

The Paimio Chair contains both two-dimensional molded plywood and laminated wood. Because of the latter's greater strength, laminated strips circled on both sides of the scrolled plywood which formed the chair's seat/back. One straight laminated crossbar in the upper back stabilized this framework. A sheet of 6.3-mm (¼") plywood sufficed in strength for the seat/back surface. Connections were made at the ends of the plywood scrolls, to their laminated supports. The scrolls themselves, the design's most characteristic feature (whence came an alternative name for the chair—the Scroll Chair) were not for decoration. They were Aalto's version of a coil spring, and added extra resiliency to the plywood design. Air vents were provided in the upper part of the back, again not for decoration, but to ventilate the user's neck, the only part of the body that might come in direct contact with the chair's lacquered surface.

The architecture of the Paimio Sanatorium was representative of the sober International Style of the 1920s. But though it was rationally designed, Aalto's Arm chair had already drifted with another tide—the softer, less calculated Scandinavian course. In the design's playful profile, Aalto provided a soothing distraction. With the introduction of the Paimio Chair, the normally despondent environment of such an institution was injected with Aalto's own zest for life.

FIGURE 23
The Paimio Armchair

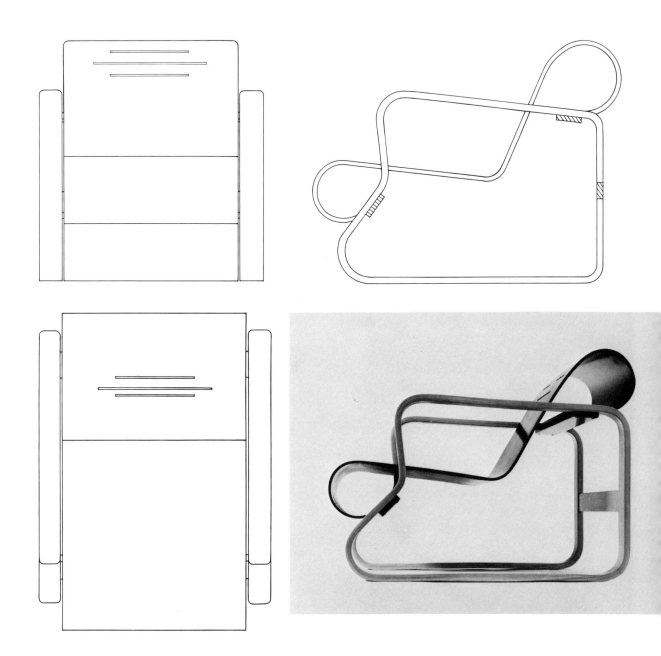

FIGURE 24

The Viipuri Tall Chair

The Viipuri Collection:
The Stacking Stool

Aalto's Viipuri Stacking Stool was a part of his scheme of furniture for the Municipal Library in Viipuri (then in Finland, now in Russia). Aalto won the project through a competition in 1927. His winning entry reflected the revival of Neoclassic styling predominant in Finland during the 1920s, but this style did not agree with the local residents. Conflicts arose over the project's contrast to its Neogothic surroundings, and the construction was delayed.

Eventually, the postponement became advantageous for Aalto. He was able to reformulate his thoughts on the library's design and to create a furniture collection for it. When construction began in 1933, a Contemporary building had replaced the original entry. The Viipuri Library was completed in 1935. Its functional plan, its lighting and acoustics, and its pacesetting interior details evidenced the architect's budding genius.

Aalto's furniture complemented the design perfectly. In 1930 he began designing this furniture based on a simple yet unique furniture joint. The innovation of the design collection was the durable and economical "Aalto leg," which bent to form a right angle that could wrap under a seat or table top and be secured with screws. Hence, the age-old problem of connecting vertical legs to horizontal surfaces was bypassed.

For his revolutionary process of forming the legs Aalto received a patent in 1935. First the upper end of a solid wooden leg was sliced along its grain, and thin glue-coated strips of wood were inserted into the grooves. Then the entire sandwich was molded to form the necessary 90-degree angle which would support the top. The entire leg could have been laminated, but a less durable element would have resulted: The exposed laminated end in contact with the floor could have splintered and separated if the stool was pulled across the floor.

FIGURE 25
The Viipuri Chair

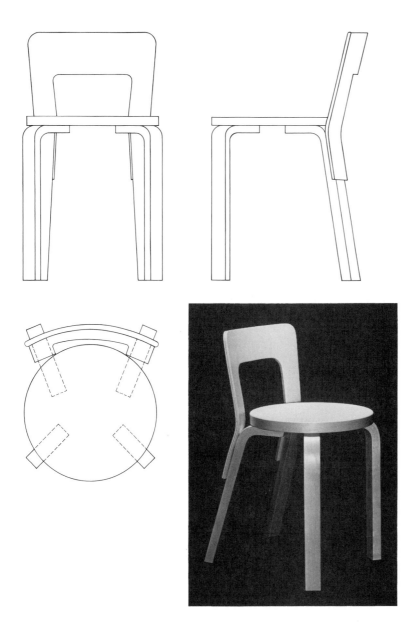

The simple, sturdy Viipuri Stacking Stool was the first piece of furniture to fully realize the effectiveness of Aalto's innovative joinery. The stool consisted of only four wooden parts: three Aalto legs and a round seat. The legs were attached to the seat at 120-degree angles, which facilitated stacking.

As was typical of Aalto's furniture, the stool was available in both adult and children's sizes. The adult size measured 350 mm (13¾") in diameter and 440 mm (17⁵⁄₁₆") high; the child's stool measured 350 mm (13¾") in diameter and 380 mm (15") high.

Varnished natural birch was used for the legs, but a variety of materials and colors were available for the seat: natural birch; birch laminated with red or black linoleum; yellow, blue, red, or white plastic laminate; and padded vinyl or raffia. The stool's durable construction and variety of finishes made it suitable for use in high-wear environments such as nurseries, schools, and public buildings.

With simple additions or substitutions of the standard parts, a wide range of stools, chairs, and tables was developed. In addition to the three-legged stool, four-legged high and low stools, side chairs with laminated backs and molded plywood backs, and a bar stool with a low plywood back were marketed. Backs were attached directly to the back legs with screws. Tables were also available, with rectangular or circular solid wooden tops. In all of the designs, the leg structure, attachment of the legs, and choice of finishes remained the same.

A major factor in Aalto's success in reintroducing wood into modern furniture design was his development of a quickly assembled, inexpensive furniture joint. The Aalto leg proved to be a most economical solution to this problem.

FIGURE 26
The Viipuri Stacking Stool

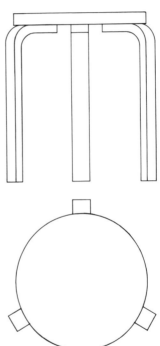

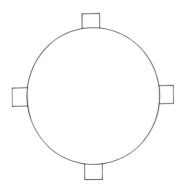

The Serving Cart

A hallmark of Aalto's furniture design career was his willingness to tackle unusual design problems. Recognizing a need for a serving cart which would fit contemporary dining habits (more relaxed and versatile meals without aid from domestic help), Aalto responded by creating a beautiful accessory for the modern home—the 1936 Serving Cart.

The first cart designed by Aalto was for his Paimio Sanatorium of 1933. This cheerful double-tiered wooden trolley eliminated the distressful clang and clatter of metal hospital carts. Its primary function in Paimio was to be used daily by the nurses in dispensing medicaments.

As was characteristic of most of the Paimio furniture, the cart's structural frame consisted of a continuous loop of two-dimensionally molded laminated birch. This frame supported the two serving shelves, the two front wheels, and the wooden handle, and also formed the two back sled feet. To move the cart forward, the feet had to be lifted from the floor, shifting the cart's weight onto the wheels. These sled feet therefore guarded against unwanted movement. A thin band of rubber capped the wheels to deaden noise.

The emphatic point of the design was the jolly bright-colored wheels. Their outer face was available in red, white, blue, yellow, or black lacquer. In later production the wheels were enlarged to their present circumference, which further increased their distinction. The shelves were veneered with white or black linoleum. Aalto's standard clear varnish finished the remaining surfaces.

In 1936 Aalto reworked the cart's design. He kept the framework, wheels, and handle, but remodeled the original to create a cart specifically suited for home use. Its looks alone were a gastronomical delight. This new design had only one shelf but compensated by providing a deep willow basket for storing tall items, such as bottles, which were not stable on the shelf during movement. This basket was inserted under the back edge of the shelf and the cart's handle. The remaining shelf was made wider and more serviceable with the addition of a deeper edge. The removal of the lower shelf was in itself an improvement because it facilitated walking.

The cart measured 900 mm (35½") long, 650 mm (25⅝") wide, and 600 mm (23⅝") high.

Aalto further enhanced this second design by harmonizing a wider range of materials and textures. The natural beauty of the wood was set off by the glossy lacquer of the wheels, the sixteen 150 mm (5⅞") ceramic tiles which veneered the shelf's top, and the fine weaving of the willow basket.

The 1936 Serving Cart anticipated the rich array of surfaces found in one of Aalto's architectural masterpieces—the 1938–1939 Villa Mairea. The cart was used in the residence, where its materials harmonized with the parquet and smooth tile floors, the columns wrapped with willow reeds, and the warm wood ceilings and walls. The freshness coupled with vitality found in both of these designs represented one of the most captivating aspects of Aalto's work.

FIGURE 27
The Aalto Serving Cart

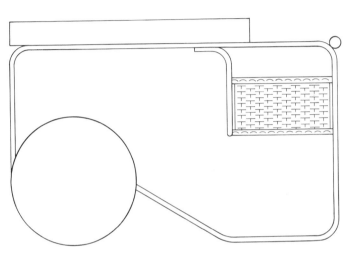

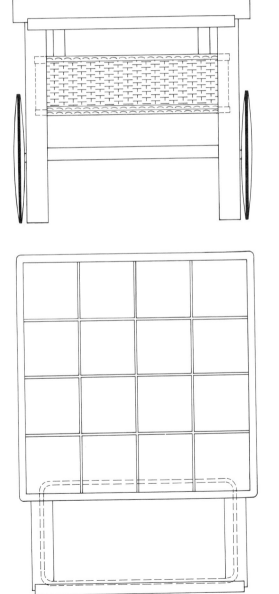

The 1946 Cantilevered Arm Chair

An outstanding contribution to twentieth-century furniture design was Aalto's successful cantilevered chair with a laminated wooden base. Since Mart Stam's introduction of this modern construction feature in the mid-1920s, steel had been the only material considered strong enough for its execution. By 1929, however, Aalto had become convinced that laminated wood also had sufficient strength to support a cantilevered seat.

The pioneering applications of the cantilever principle were familiar to Aalto. He had access to current journals and catalogs in addition to firsthand knowledge from his travel experiences. Aalto had visited Holland and France in 1928 (the same year he ordered several pieces of Breuer's furniture from Gebrüder Thonet for use in his own home). Then, in 1929, he attended the *Congrès Internationaux d'Architecture Moderne* (CIAM), in Frankfurt, Germany, which assembled the major leaders of the International Style. Inspired by these contacts, Aalto returned home to design a cantilevered chair of tubular steel with a molded plywood seat and an all-wood prototype with a laminated frame. His first attempts were unsuccessful, but four years of continued research culminated in a stable design—the 1933 Cantilevered Arm Chair, first used in the Paimio Sanatorium. The structural framework of this seminal design set a pattern for his later models, of which the webbed 1946 Cantilevered Arm Chair, Model No. 406, became the most renowned.

Aalto's original cantilevered chair of 1929–1933 consisted of a thin, 6.3-mm (¼") molded plywood seat surface resting on a frame of laminated wood. The frame was composed of two C-shaped supporting side members that were connected with horizontal braces at the curving front and upper back. These braces also served as the foundation to which the seat/back was attached. The laminated parts of the design received a clear varnish finish; the molded plywood was available in clear varnish and colored lacquer finishes.

The success of Aalto's design hinged on the ability of the laminated base to provide the necessary stability. Because stress was greatest on the lower, supporting half of the framework, Aalto constructed a lamination of seven layers just below the front edge of the seat. The entire arm segment was thinner in profile because extra reinforcement was not required there.

The process of construction was as well planned as the design. The curved laminated parts were sliced from a preformed sandwiched sheet of birch veneers. The supporting strips for several chairs could thus be obtained from one molding process. The same was true of the seat/back surface. A stack of plywood sheets was pressed together as one unit, with paper placed between the sheets, so that the molded components were easily separated after the pressing.

FIGURE 28

The 1946 Cantilevered Armchair

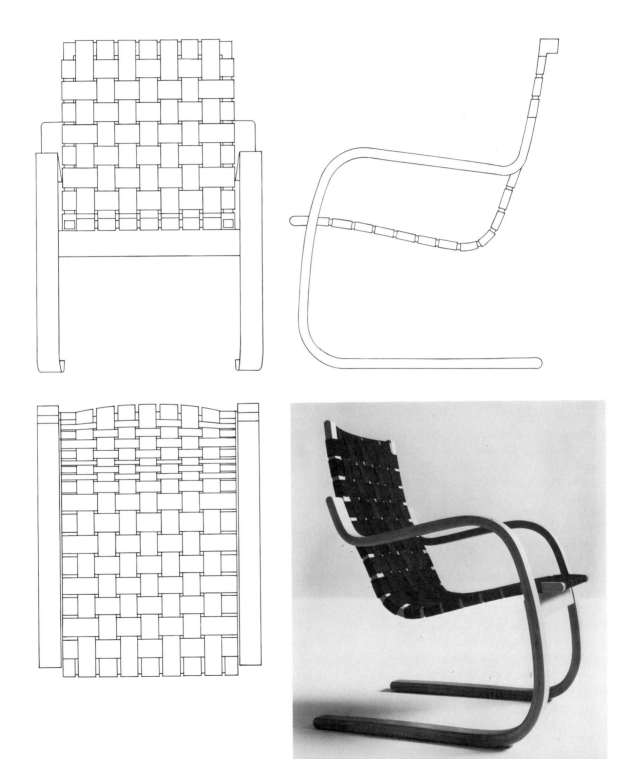

Aalto was not satisfied with this early design. He replaced the plywood seat with more comfortable surfaces, and introduced models with foam-cushioned seats, backs, and even padded head rests, while keeping the original cantilevered base design. Other cantilevered supports were introduced in a heavily upholstered chair in 1936 and a chaise longue with webbed upholstery in 1937. The 1946 Arm Chair reintroduced the 1933 support, with a seat frame and upholstery that allowed more comfortable seating than the two-dimensionally molded plywood of the first design. No improvements were needed on the pacesetting 1933 cantilevered supporting frame.

Although the original arm chair has been discontinued, Aalto's 1946 remake has met with wide acceptance due to its more resilient, formfitting seating surface. The frame gently undulates to conform to the human backbone, and the chair's back extends higher than on the earlier plywood model to give more support to the upper back and neck. On the 1946 chair, 50-mm (2") cotton webbing was interlaced on the frame and attached with screws—an upholstery technique popular with Aalto at this time, which he had used for lounges such as his 1936 design and for the upholstery of stools. Today the 1946 Cantilevered Arm chair is available with black, brown, or natural cotton webbing; rattan; or of vinyl, leather, or canvas quilting. The entire framework is of laminated birch finished with clear varnish.

The chair measures 600 mm (23⅝") wide, 720 mm (28⁵⁄₁₆") deep, and 880 mm (34⅝") high, with a seat height of 400 mm (15¾").

Aalto placed much importance on the continuum of design. Designs did not emerge fully matured like Athena from the head of Zeus. Designing, like all aspects of life, developed and focused with the passing of time. Culminating in this last design, the 1946 Arm Chair, the history of Aalto's cantilevered furniture is an example of this philosophy applied to the furniture design process, and offers proof of its validity.

The 1954 Fan Leg Stool

The 1954 Fan Leg Stool was a splendid member of Aalto's furniture portfolio. Its mellifluous lines resulted from the organic technique used to connect the seat with the legs: The fan, or so-called X-shaped leg, jointed directly into the side of the top. The beautiful fanning detail manifested the structural possibilities and natural beauty of the wood. Both Aalto and his clientele considered this piece to be the most beautiful product of his search for modern furniture joints.

The groundwork of the fan leg was laid by Aalto in earlier innovations. The first had been the Aalto leg for the furniture of the 1935 Viipuri Library. Then, in 1947, the "little sister to the column," Aalto's term for his Y-shaped leg, was constructed from two of the Viipuri leg designs. This new leg separated at the top to outline and form the frame of two adjacent sides of the seat or table top, instead of bending under it. With the fan-shaped joint, a more delicate unity between vertical and horizontal planes was created.

The three-legged round stool was the simplest member of the "X" 600 Fan Series. We believe it to be the exemplary classic of the entire

FIGURE 29

The 1954 Fan Leg Stool

collection. The leg, the most significant element in all of Aalto's furniture, consisted of five wedge-shaped "Aalto legs," combined to form a single column which fanned out at the top. They were joined to the seat with dowels and glue. In order to conform to the fanning contour of the leg, the seat was arched at the point of attachment. As was not true of Aalto's previous groups of furniture, the complexity of assembling and attaching this multimembered design resulted in a costly product.

The round Fan Leg Stool measured 380 mm (15") round and 440 mm (17⁵⁄₁₆") high.

Square, four-legged stools as well as hexagonal, three-legged stools were also included in the group. A natural ash seat was standard, but padded and upholstered seats with vinyl or leather could also be obtained. The legs were of laminated birch. When the design was first introduced, tables were available with ash, oak, or glass tops. Today, glass is no longer available.

The fanlike or radiating shape, the decorative structural element of the group, was also found in Aalto's architecture of this period. At the same time as the Fan Leg group was introduced, Aalto was working on the main building for the University of Technology in Ontaniemi, Finland. Both his sketches of interiors and drafted plans incorporated this fanning detail. Later examples included the House of Culture Concert Hall plan in Helsinki (1958); the plan and auditorium of the Culture Center in Wolfsburg, West Germany (1958–1962); and the plan of the Bremen Apartment House, West Germany (1963).

Yet this furniture detail did not originate as an architectonic feature; it was adopted from couture. The Fan Leg Stool made its first appearance in a small exhibit of Aalto's work at the Nordiska Kompaniet department store of Stockholm in 1954. A personal friend in charge of the event encouraged Aalto to present "something new." He designed and introduced the stool for the showing, and presented one of the originals to the young woman whose plissé skirt had been the inspiration for his new creation.

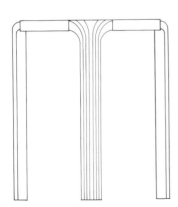
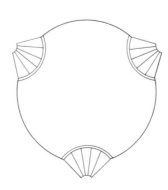

6

Hans J. Wegner

Hans J. Wegner affirmed the place of handcrafted perfection in the spectrum of twentieth-century furniture design. His furniture represents an aspect of traditional design which had been neglected throughout the century. But Wegner in no way compromised the foundation of Contemporary design philosophy. He employed the most appropriate materials and production techniques available to produce functional and aesthetically pleasing designs.

Unlike the majority of European designers of the 1900s, Wegner was not faced by shortages of solid wood and affordable skilled labor. Denmark was a country of craftsmen and abundant hardwood forests. Even after World War II, it was not considered a fully industrialized nation. Given this situation, Wegner's solution was most appropriate. He knew the assets and the limits of his region's industry, and demanded the precision which was possible only through handcrafting.

Bored with the misuse of "machine styling" typical at mid-century, the consumers of industrialized countries welcomed this relief from machine furniture. Wegner's smooth, warm materials and styling became a gentle balm for the fast-paced chaos of Western life.

Hans Jørgensen Wegner was born on April 2, 1914, in Tønder, a small city bordering Germany in the Jutland region of southern Denmark. In Tønder he was surrounded with skilled craftsmen on whose services the townspeople still depended. His father was a shoemaker. Only two houses away lived the town's cabinetmaker, to whom the young Hans went to ask for scraps of wood to play with. Though the pride and skill of his father and the other local craftsmen impressed Wegner, he later realized that his mother made the greatest contribution to his career. She "understood things" and encouraged her son to develop and refine his aesthetic awareness. By his mid-teens he had developed the talent of wood sculpting. Carvings from this period evidenced his respect for and understanding of the material, and his care in molding it into something beautiful.

At the age of 13 Wegner began a four-year apprenticeship in a local Tønder cabinet shop. There he learned the basics of constructing all types of furniture and fittings. During this time he began toying with the possibility of eventually opening his own workshop. It seemed logical that, with the quantity of poorly designed furniture growing in Denmark, he was assured of a successful career if he could produce good furniture. With this goal he left home in 1936 to further refine his skills at the Danish Institute of Technology in Copenhagen. Later he enrolled in the Copenhagen School of Arts and Crafts, the leading advanced education center for workshop masters at the time.

At the Copenhagen School of Arts and Crafts, Wegner's studies comprehended an overview of the visual fine arts: drawing, painting, sculpting, and art history. As a student in furniture design, he was required to measure and draw examples of traditional furniture in the Arts and Crafts Museum's collection. A fine art instructor was so impressed with Wegner's painting skills that he tried to convince him to change his course of study; he would make a much better living with the more reliable profession of a portrait painter. After all, until then nobody had been able to make a living as a designer of Modern furniture.

Since the late 1920s the Danish markets had been flooded with cheap furniture imports. This competition, coupled with the mass-produced products of domestic industry, caused a decline in the cabinetmaker's profession. In addition to these marketing problems, the typical homeowner still preferred poor copies of period pieces over well-designed Contemporary furniture.

But Wegner persisted. His furniture design teacher, O. Moelgaard Nielsen, encouraged him and eventually recommended him to Arne Jacobsen, a famous Danish architect at that time. While still a student, Wegner designed some furniture for Jacobsen's personal summer residence. Then in 1938, with Moelgaard Nielsen's blessing, he left school to work full-time in the drawing office of Arne Jacobsen and Erik Moeller.

Wegner's main project for these architects was designing the furniture for the town hall of Aarhus (capital of Jutland). These designs were founded on the "traditions of craftsmanship and the moral influence" which the Danish design reformer Kaare Klint embodied. Already, during the late 1920s, Klint had directed the course of Danish Contemporary design with his concepts of functional form. As a professor of the Royal Academy of Architecture, he had encouraged his students to study and rework successful design solutions of the past, especially English furniture of the eighteenth century. Though never a student of Klint, Wegner knew of his work; Klint's approach was well known during Wegner's student days and was a frequent topic of discussion. But Wegner's design career was not to be restrained by the past or by a lack of personal artistic initiative. Even in his early student work, Wegner's Aarhus designs incorporated a much-advanced "language of form"—a sculptural sensitivity—which was later to become the basis of modern Danish furniture design.

The 1940s might well have been the most significant decade of Wegner's career. During these years his design philosophy crystallized and the impact of his designs spread abroad.

Success began promptly in 1940. While

working in Jacobsen's office, Wegner met Inga Helbo. They were married on November 9, 1940. The same year he also met the second most important person in his life, Johannes Hansen.

Hansen was a well-established and respected Danish cabinetmaker, one of the founders of the Danish Cabinetmakers' Guild exhibitions. Founded in Copenhagen in 1926 by a group of twenty-five professional cabinetmakers, the guild's aim was to promote public and architectural interest in the genuine beauty of superbly crafted furniture. But the guild performed an even more important function. Its annual exhibitions became a meeting point for progressive designers, and its members greatly benefited from interaction with the architectural design community. Wegner had been associated with the group for two years and was a promising 26-year-old when he and Hansen met. His creativity impressed Hansen. Out of mutual respect they formed a designer/ manufacturer association which lasted until the elder's death in 1961 and continues today with his son, Poul Hansen.

German troops invaded Denmark on April 9, 1940. During the ensuing five-year occupation, the momentum of the design community faltered because of the shortage of materials and unstable economic conditions resulting from Denmark's political isolation.

Wegner completed the Aarhus project in 1942 but was unable to return to Copenhagen because of travel restrictions. In spite of this enforced idleness, he took advantage of his situation. From 1943 to 1944 he spent much of his time in the local library analyzing the

enduring beauty and function found in earlier design epochs. In particular the designs of antiquity and the Orient and many forms of provincial furniture, such as Shaker and Windsor, captured his attention. In 1944 he channeled these inspirations into his first chair for mass production, the later so-called "Chinese Chair" (consisting of four variations) which the firm of Fritz Hansen manufactured. Wegner was also accepted as a member of the Royal Association of Danish Architects. By the end of the war he had, among other things, executed detailed marquetries; experimented in lighting, flatware design, and office furniture; and designed a set of children's furniture. He entered and won several competitions before returning to Copenhagen in 1946.

A frenzy of postwar activity followed the occupation. At Moelgaard Nielsen's suggestion Wegner accepted a teaching position at his old school (he would remain with the Arts and Crafts School until 1953). His afternoons and evenings were spent in the restoration of a salvaged ship. Along with Palle Suenson, Wegner was responsible for the woodwork and furniture. In addition to this project and his teaching responsibilities, Wegner continued to concentrate on his own furniture designing. 1947 was an outstanding year: In Copenhagen, at the annual Cabinetmakers' Exhibition of that year, Wegner showed his famous Peacock Chair (Figure 30.)

This initial recognition was supplemented the following year (1948), when Wegner entered the Museum of Modern Art's International Low-Cost Furniture Competition. His molded plywood arm chair won an honorable mention and later toured the United States.

Wegner's Guild Exhibits of 1949 and 1953 further confirmed his place in the history of design. The Classic Chair, sometimes referred to as *The* Chair (Figure 31), and the Folding Chair (Figure 32) were introduced in 1949. These chairs were shown along with his Peacock chair of 1947 in *Interiors* and *House Beautiful.* The Classic Chair was acclaimed by both the public and the critics in the Good Design Exhibition in Chicago. By 1953, when the Valet Chair (Figure 33) appeared, Wegner's international fame was well established.

These postwar masterworks were visually lightweight, unobtrusive designs in which form was reduced to pure essentials. Their sculptural lines were hand-carved from solid wood: domestic oak or ash, or imported teak. Then the wood was sanded and finished with oil or wax. These natural finishes not only enhanced the wood's tactile warmth, but in time would darken slightly to form a fine patina. Wegner's furniture reflected the quality of workmanship which his profession took pride in and established him as an eminent leader of the new spirit of design from Denmark.

Today, at his home studio in Gentofte, a suburb of Copenhagen, Wegner continues to design *The* chair, *The* table, and *The* cabinet. In

the late 1940s he was once described as not being very prolific. The description is certainly dated. Wegner has designed with solid wood, molded plywood, laminated wood, and steel, creating residential, dormitory, conference, office, and hospital furniture—practically everything from sewing baskets to speakers' stands.

Throughout his career, however, Wegner has given considerable time and emphasis to the designing of seating furniture. The profusion of chair designs originating from his office and their effectiveness in modern environments bear witness to his concern. Wegner's design theory has been a practical one: A chair should provide comfortable, healthy seating. Observing his human subject, he established guidelines for reaching this goal.

In his years of contemplating the human form, Wegner drew an important conclusion: Sitting was basically a human invention, a compromise between standing and lying down. Even under the best conditions, sitting was likely to be awkward for the body; it required shifting of weight to maintain a suitable degree of comfort. Therefore, Wegner made roomy designs, with rounded back rails that allowed numerous changes of position. According to his observations, sitting people searched for a place to rest their arms. Since arm rests relieved the full load of the body's weight from the spine, they became another essential in Wegner's handiwork. All of his chairs were capable of comfortably containing the squirming, fidgety, ever-shifting contemporary body.

Just as there was no one chair perfect for the many varied activities of the day, Wegner also realized that there was no one chair to fit every body type. Certain constants existed, however, which Wegner used to enable his designs to conform to the widest range of the human population. In most adults, the measurement from the small of the back to the tip of the seat bone is basically the same. Wegner's chairs for upright sitting reflected this fact in the placement of the supportive rail for the back. Moreover, Wegner often left the space under the rail open so that the sitter could "get his bottom into the chair" for a proper upright body position. Surmising that a tall person could sit in a low chair more comfortably than a short person could manage a higher one, he designed chairs with seat heights lower than standard.

Wegner's concepts were developed and often tested in his own home before being considered for manufacturing. From his preliminary sketches he built scaled models in order to test a design's composition and to smooth out technical problems. In this way refinements in form could be made quickly and production costs and time estimated. Next came one or more full-scale models quickly constructed from pine or plywood. With these working models further corrections were easily made. Then, Wegner frequently constructed a prototype which his family tried at home. When the design was approved, detailed manufacturer's drawings were compiled, and production began under Wegner's supervision.

Originally Wegner created furniture specifically for either mass production or hand production. Large manufacturers such as Fritz Hansen produced his machine designs; the smaller firm of Johannes Hansen built those which required handcrafting. Today, however, even in Johannes Hansen's production of such sculptural masterpieces as the Classic Chair, machines have replaced much of the hand labor.

Mr. Wegner is a gentle, reserved, soft-featured man. As a host, he is the embodiment of Danish hospitality. His unassuming attitude toward his life and work is most impressive. When asked if he had apprenticed early as a young boy or received other forms of preparatory training, he lowered his head and softly replied, "No." Then, raising his eyes, he added in a gently mischievous manner, "I played!"—not at all the reply one would expect from a designer of such stature.

Yet this attitude is sensed throughout his career. Not that his work came easily; on the contrary, many of Wegner's concepts required years to perfect. Now they are found in museum collections and have an international market, but this renown is not his source of pride. As a dedicated craftsman he strives for perfection in his art. For this, Wegner enjoys the peace and confidence of one who is pleased with his life's work.

The Peacock Chair

Hans J. Wegner's Peacock Chair has become a symbol of Contemporary Danish furniture. It simultaneously embodied all of Wegner's integral design concerns. He designed the chair in 1947 and first exhibited it that year at the annual Danish Cabinetmakers' Guild show in Copenhagen. In 1949 the chair was again shown at the annual exhibition, and this time it received international attention. Its cordial fireside appearance has since made it one of the most well known and loved of all Wegner's pieces.

The fundamental makeup of Wegner's Peacock Chair was based on that of the earlier Windsor Chair. This lightweight, durable provincial design had been popular in both England and America since the early eighteenth century. As in traditional Windsor styling, the seat of the Peacock Chair was the common connecting point of all of the chair's back members as well as for the legs and arm supports. The chair back consisted of a large hoop—the chair's most characteristic feature—which held sixteen radiating spindles. The four splayed legs were braced with side stretchers and a centered cross-stretcher. These supporting elements were simple, straight turnings which thickened at points of connection, a trait typified in the original Windsor designs.

At first glance, the Peacock Chair could easily be mistaken for its traditional forerunner. Closer inspection, however, reveals the distinctions of its Danish designer.

Into the traditional form Wegner integrated new elements of comfort, durability, and nobility. The fourteen cattail-shaped spindles in the back were not merely decorative elements; each was carefully carved with subtle variations to conform to the user's back. The chair also included two other comfort elements both typical of Wegner's furniture: a scale large enough to provide room for shifting one's sitting position, and a resilient woven seat. For extra strength and stability, Wegner used a solid piece of laminated wood instead of bentwood for the back hoop. A solid rod of ash was sliced into four strips, then laminated back together and shaped. With this construction technique, better control could be maintained during the molding process, assuring a smooth, even curve. Except for the arms, all members of the chair were made of ash and finished with wax. The arms Wegner purposely made of teak, and finished with oil; over the years the natural oils from the owner's skin would enhance the look of the teak. This insistence on minimal finishes allowed the entire piece to gather a patina not possible with harder finishes.

The measurements of the Peacock Chair are 770 mm (30⅞") wide, 770 mm (30⅞") deep, and 1,030 mm (40⅞") high.

The Peacock Chair has been widely publicized. Of the hundreds of pictures and articles that have appeared in trade and professional journals, the two most famous were published in 1949 and 1974. The first showed Queen Ingrid, of Denmark gracefully sitting in the chair at the Danish Cabinetmakers Guild show. This royal attention brought hundreds of orders for the chair from around the world. Twenty-five years later, when *National*

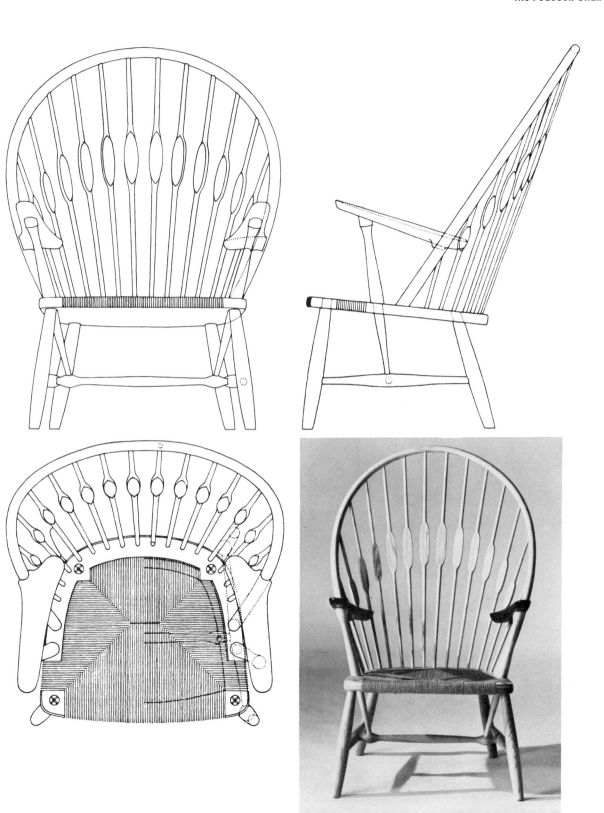

FIGURE 30
The Peacock Chair

Geographic was doing a feature article on Denmark, the Peacock Chair was chosen as representative of the country's furniture industry and was pictured with its famous designer.

The name "Peacock" came as a direct translation of the Danish name for the chair, *Paafugl.* Wegner, the humble craftsman did not give it this name; it came from his public. Although the term might derive from the chair's fanning back, it even more aptly describes the proud feelings of the chair's owner toward his new purchase.

The Classic Chair

The machine advocates of the early twentieth century were rather perturbed by Wegner's Classic Chair of 1949. It was designed for hand labor, made of solid wood, and traditionally joined, yet had an intriguing simplicity that had seldom been conceived before. The same descriptive slogans used with the earlier Rational furniture justly appraised Wegner's craft: Purism, Functionalism, "Less is more"; but Wegner's interpretation represented a different tempo of modern life. The sculptural knitting of the chair's parts was unprecedented in earlier Contemporary design and heralded the Danish trend to come.

Throughout Wegner's career, he took great care to avoid current trends, both domestic and international. Even as a student, he realized that the major job of a designer was not assimilating influences but trying not to be ruled by them. This interpretive principle applied to academic training as well—he believed that it should prompt, not guide a student's direction.

Nevertheless, the past was not to be ignored. After all, Wegner's private study during Denmark's occupation had inspired his unique personal course. But the foremost influence on Wegner, which would serve as both the means and the end of the Classic Chair's design, was the traditional Danish concern for quality.

Because Denmark has always been a small country with few natural resources, the Danes have long recognized that quality, not quantity, is their best competitive lever on the world market. The modeling of raw materials developed into a major occupation, and success depended on good workmanship. This value was implanted in Wegner's earliest memories. Disgusted with the inferior productions of the first part of the century, Wegner determined to prove that Danish craftsmen could still produce high quality. His Classic Chair became a monument to Danish skill.

Unlike traditional handcraftsmen, Wegner did not busy himself with surface decoration or unnecessary embellishments of the design. Instead the refined form and enticing display of each material's natural beauty became the chair's emphatic points.

As evidenced in its basic form and, in particular, its curving back rail, the Classic Chair was an offspring of an earlier Wegner design—the 1944 Chinese Chair. But Wegner's 1949 model contained a sophisticated sculptural refinement all its own. The curving back extended into slender arm rests and smoothly attached to the four gently splaying legs. Like the arms, the legs were shaped to conform to function; they thickened at the point

FIGURE 31
The Classic Chair

of attachment to the seat rails and then tapered to the floor. But despite its economy of form, the chair was comfortable to sit in. Without the bulk of padding, its arms and back were sculptured to fit the body in a variety of sitting positions. Moreover, the caning of the seat attached to a bowed front seat rail, which also facilitated comfort. Oak or teak was used for the chair's wooden frame, finished with oil or wax, respectively. The caning was handwoven from selected Indonesian rattan.

The dimensions of the Classic Chair are 570 mm (22⅜") wide, 460 mm (18⅛") deep, and 762 mm (30") high, with a seat height of 430 mm (17").

In its thirty-year history, the chair has undergone only slight modifications. The first came very shortly after the prototype had been accepted for production. During a visit to Johannes Hansen's workshop, Wegner reconsidered the shape of the arm. Making the arm taper more gently, he sketched his revision directly onto the working drawings. This version remains on today's market.

Later, another modification occurred—one that especially pleased its designer. In his original design Wegner had used exposed mortise and tenon joints to connect the three-piece back rail. With aging and changes of humidity this joint had a tendency to separate slightly. Another disadvantage was that the rectangular outline of the joint detracted from the sculptural lines of the chair. So Wegner wrapped the back of the design with rattan in order to conceal these disadvantages and achieve a more aesthetic effect. However, a year later, in 1950, Wegner successfully

employed a saw-tooth joint. Its zigzag shape eliminated both of the earlier problems, and the dishonest rattan wrapping was abandoned, except for special orders.

Because of the differences in humidity between Denmark and parts of the United States, an upholstered variation of the chair was introduced. It had been discovered that the caned seat could sag in American use; therefore a padded leather seat was made available. When discussing this change, Wegner expressed his personal feelings: "If consumers use their head, they will specify leather; but if they use their heart, they will take their chances with the original caned seat."

The name "Classic Chair" was not Wegner's title; he had called it the "Round Chair." He arrived at this term because of the chair's basic plan and the soft contours of its members; there were no sharp angles in the design. Its present name originated from English-speaking admirers who were so enthralled with the design that they called it "*The* Chair." Wegner discounts "*The* Chair," reasoning that in 1949, at age 35, he surely had not reached the apex of chair design. Like a father, Wegner prides in all of his "children"; but one cannot help sensing that no matter what the title, this design is his career favorite.

The Folding Chair

The challenges involved in designing a folding chair fascinated Hans J. Wegner for a long time. His earliest attempt was in 1937; however, this design was never manufactured. His successful 1949 Folding Chair was produced after its

FIGURE 32
The Folding Chair

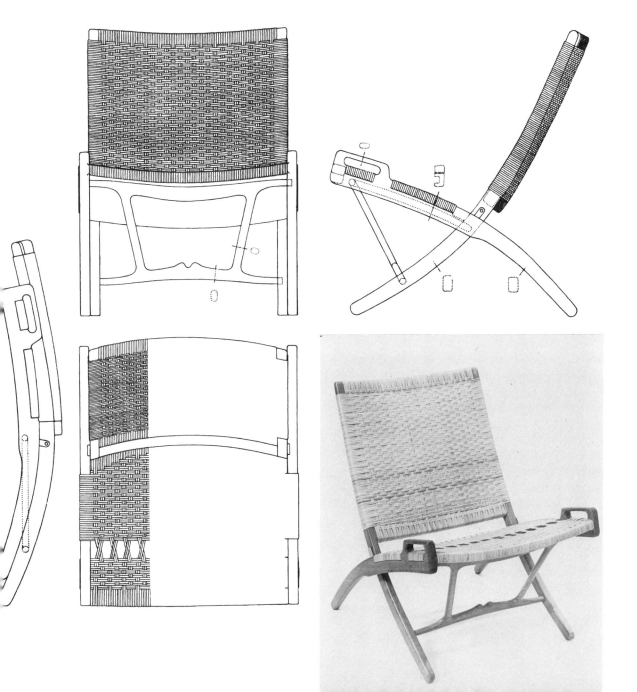

debut in the annual Danish Cabinetmakers' Guild Exhibition.

Wegner had always felt justified in this pursuit. In his opinion, one could never have enough additional seating. The practical convenience of having an extra chair that could be easily folded and stored when not in use appealed to the master, as did the mechanics of its function.

To be sure, a lengthy history preceded Wegner's Folding Chair. It was not the first design to employ the time-proven dynamics of triangular construction—the basis of X-shaped folding furniture. Transportable folding stools have capitalized on this pressure resistance system since prehistoric times. Before the Renaissance these stools were used primarily by the wealthy when traveling. During the fifteenth and sixteenth centuries backs were incorporated, and designs such as the Italian Savonarola could be found in homes of all classes throughout Europe. In recent centuries use of folding stools and chairs has been more or less limited to outdoor activities.

Due to its light weight, wood has remained the dominant construction material throughout the history of folding furniture, though metal designs have also been produced. In both cases the seat, which was usually of canvas, leather, or wood, tied together and was supported on the tops of the crisscrossed legs. The design's triangular support, therefore, consisted of the upper half of the legs and the seat. To achieve balance, this function and

arrangement dictated that the seat surface be flat and horizontal.

Wegner made several changes in the traditional arrangement which resulted in substantial improvements. The major change consisted of a better distribution of body weight. Wegner's supporting triangular construction incorporated the seat surface, the front leg, and the seat's front brace. The brace, which carried pressure from the seat almost directly to the floor, was the distinction of Wegner's design. This unique reorganization allowed a lower sloping position for both the seat and back surfaces. A chair that was more relaxing and more stable than previous folding chairs was the result.

Wegner's seat brace was also vital in the storage of the chair. To close the chair, the front edge of the seat and the chair's back were lifted and drawn together. This action freed the supporting brace and allowed its upper end to glide along the inside frame of the seat, until it eventually rested flush against the collapsed seat and back sections. Thus compacted, the chair could be turned upside down and hung on the wall with a special hook that conformed to the notch of the brace's cross-stretcher.

The Folding Chair measures 610 mm (24") wide, 470 mm (18½") deep, and 750 mm (29½") high.

Due to their mechanical requirements, folding chairs generally have not been noted for their comfort and outstanding beauty. Wegner's interpretation is an exception. Instead of serving only as seating for overflow crowds, his chair is usually a permanent part of an interior scheme. It has none of the stigma normally attached to folding furniture. It is a substantial design, with a relaxing, visually delightful form.

When asked to expound on his Folding Chair's history, Wegner points out that in all of his designs, the design process is too spontaneous and interdependent an operation for him to single out which aspects had preponderance. He seldom rationalizes a design's success or analyzes its influences. Though artistic inspiration is important to Wegner, he believes that success is more dependent on the skill and integrity of the craftsman. Therefore he prefers to speak of his Folding Chair in terms of its carved perfection, the beauty of its naturally finished oak and rattan, and its uniquely successful operation.

The Valet Chair

The 1951 Valet Chair was a design indulgence, Wegner's solution to a minor but perplexing problem. The days of the manservant were over, so a modern-day gentleman needed a convenient place to hang his clothes before going to bed. Wegner decided to create a chair that would fulfill this purpose. The result was a sensibly detailed, well-executed design in the Wegner tradition.

Though fanciful in appearance, the Valet Chair was the epitome of practicality. Having observed that a normal chair back deformed a jacket's shoulders, Wegner designed the top rail so that a jacket could drape correctly, as on a coat hanger. The seat height and angle was perfect for removing shoes. Hinged in front, the seat could be raised 90 degrees forward; in this position, it became a functional rack on which a man could hang his trousers. Moreover, a convenient cache under this seat/rack was provided for storing pocket contents and jewelry. When used as a chair while removing or putting on socks and shoes, the formfitting wooden seat and back provided a convenient and surprisingly comfortable sitting position.

These features were packaged in a compact design that measured 508 mm (20") wide, 495 mm (19½") deep, and 939 mm (37") high.

The three-legged Valet Chair consisted of two front legs and a center back leg. The back leg extended to form the foundation of the curved chair back and to support the hanger-shaped top rail. In the sitting position the seat rested on the two front legs and the cache's framework, which it concealed. Sufficient space between the raised seat and the cache allowed a pair of pants to drape through freely. A stretcher braced the front legs, and the cache framework connected the back leg to the front legs of the chair.

The original design shown in 1953 was altered before going into production. When first conceived, the Valet Chair had four legs, but Wegner was not pleased with the design. Even when King Frederick IX ordered one of these chairs, he was kept waiting eighteen months while Wegner simplified and improved the design. Eventually, a back leg was eliminated; the chair thus became easier to walk around when hanging up a coat. Both Wegner and the King were pleased. The King began ordering the chairs as gifts for his friends, and to this day, Wegner—like many other commoners—continues to use the Valet Chair in his own bedroom.

FIGURE 33
The Valet Chair

The Post-World War II American Scene

After decades of copying design tendencies from abroad, America finally made its first solid contribution to the Contemporary camp with its innovative postwar designs.

For many Americans, mention of interiors during the 1940s and 1950s conjures up memories of blond furniture with tapering legs, sectional sofas, and kidney-shaped cocktail tables. Colors were pastel and small geometric patterns were the dominant prints for textiles and wallpapers. Frequently, room furnishings were oriented toward the picture window, which in many cases revealed a pastoral front lawn set with birdbaths surrounded by statues of pink flamingos. Scandinavian furniture, or the popular American copies known as ''Danish Modern,'' was in great demand, along with such new organic designs as the amorphous creations of the sculptor Isamu Noguchi. And so America shied away from the reminders of the war years.

The steel classics of the 1920s were temporarily forgotten—but not for long. By the late 1950s and early 1960s, the international trend had changed from natural materials and informal interiors to the sober, serene look of the ''Minimal Style.'' The reintroduction of the works of the original masters, Mies van der Rohe in particular, generated waves of chrome-plated furniture and tufted leather upholstery. Forms were crisp and geometric. The Rational viewpoint was further augmented with new compositions by Florence Knoll in the United States, Poul Kjaerholm in Denmark, and Robert Haussmann in Switzerland. Once again, the order and regularity of the initial Contemporary course found acceptance.

The innovative American designs of the postwar period did not favor either of these design extremes, but successfully integrated aspects of each. As with tubular steel and molded laminated wood previously, new technology generated a design challenge. The softer, organic forms of Scandinavia were recreated using the latest developments of American technical science—an abundance of new materials and the new processes which made them applicable and affordable in furniture construction.

Charles Eames and Eero Saarinen became the undisputed leaders of this new development in international design. Their research before and after the war produced a new concept in furniture structure: the three-dimensional molded shell. This thin, durable, organic structure could be formed from a wide range of materials, such as molded plywood, metal, plastic, and wire lattice. Eames and Saarinen also reintroduced vivid colors—not used in furniture since Reitveld designs—into the Contemporary movement. Many designers followed their lead: George Nelson and Harry Bertoia in America and the Dane Arne Jacobsen were the best known during the 1950s.

The scores of new design possibilities revealed by Eames and Saarinen were also not wasted on the inventive generation of designers in the following decade. During the 1960s dynamic design repercussions resulted not only from the synthetic materials and revolutionary constructions which Eames and Saarinen pioneered, but also from the new concept of furniture which these innovations made possible.

Eames and Saarinen began to challenge the very definition of furniture, in particular its form. Consequently, the creations of their successors were more understandable.

7

Charles Eames

Charles Eames, an American, emerged as the creative genius of the post-World War II design community. A diligent designer, he solved problems in an impressive range of disciplines: furniture design, filmmaking, graphic art, photography, and education—all with expertise. Problems in these areas required structural solutions; and Eames therefore believed he never left his trained vocation of architecture. Greatly aided by Ray Eames, his partner and wife, he gave new aesthetic and technical dimensions to the phrase "Form follows function."

Eames had no formal alignment with any design movement. He neither gave sermons on design reform nor worked in a particular shape or construction technique, and he had no motto. To design a chair, he researched a particular human need and concerned himself with its solution. With rigorous attention to detail, he created the production process and adopted suitable materials. The array of materials which he combined and used included aluminum, steel, molded plywood, fiberglass, reinforced plastic, foam rubber, natural down, and even pony skin. No single look, material, or culture linked his designs

together. Viewed as a whole, Eames's furniture lacked apparent continuity; he believed that every object should have its own integrity. This approach to furniture, with each piece designed in light of its own space and time, made up the so-called "Eames Aesthetic." Yet, whether in groups or separately, his furniture pieces were most versatile, suitable for residential and commercial environments worldwide.

Charles Eames was born on June 17, 1907, in St. Louis, Missouri. His father, an amateur artist and photographer, died in 1919. At age 13, the disciplined young Eames first experimented with photography, following the directions on his father's wetplate equipment. Through this primitive technique he taught himself the art. During the summers of his high school years, he worked at Laclide Steel Company in Venice, Illinois. Eventually, he became a draftsman for the company. A popular personality, he was elected captain of the football team and president of his senior class at Yeatman High School. After winning a scholarship to study architecture, he became president of the freshman class at Washington University in St. Louis, Missouri. But he caused dismay to the architectural faculty. As a student he was captivated by the work of Frank Lloyd Wright. His teachers, on the other hand, were still using the principles of the Academy of Beaux Arts. Eames left the university after two years, but always counted himself fortunate to have had two years of Beaux Arts training.

Undaunted by his teachers' disapproval, Eames worked from 1925 to 1928 for an architectural firm, Trueblood and Graf. By 1929 he had saved enough money to travel. His trip to Europe, where the Modern movement began, gave him a firsthand look at works of Contemporary masters which had remained at the 1927 site of the Weissenhof Exhibition in Stuttgart. He returned home enthusiastic, and in 1930 opened his own architectural firm, Gray and Eames. Since architectural commissions were rare in the Depression years, Eames branched into other areas as extensions of building projects—renovation, designing lighting fixtures, rugs, stained glass windows and ecclesiastical vestments, and pottery.

Eames's work drew the attention of Eliel Saarinen (1873–1950), president of Cranbrook Academy of Art in Bloomfield Hills, Michigan, who offered him a fellowship in 1936. Eames's associates at Cranbrook included an all-star cast: Eero Saarinen, Florence Schust (later Knoll), Harry Bertoia, Harry Weese, and Ray Kaiser, who later became his wife. All of them were to become leaders in furniture design. A year later, in 1937, Eames became head of the new department of Experimental Design at Cranbrook.

From 1938 to 1939, Eames continued teaching and also worked with Eero Saarinen in the architectural office of Saarinen's father. Collaborating, and with the assistance of Ray Kaiser, they produced the winning entries in two categories of the 1940–1941 Museum of Modern Art (MOMA) Organic Furniture competition. Their plywood chair was unique not only in its complex three-dimensional molding, but also in its use of an unprecedented furniture joint which made possible the bonding of wood to rubber to metal. The priorities of impending war prevented this chair from being marketed.

In 1941 Charles Eames and Ray Kaiser married. They moved to a Richard Neutra apartment in southern California. MGM had employed Eames as a set designer; *Arts and Architecture* hired Ray as a cover designer. Moonlighting at home, the two developed mass production techniques for making molded plywood furniture, designing and building the needed equipment themselves: homemade autoclave, presses, and molds.

Applying their research toward the war effort, the Eameses developed molded plywood splints and received a commission from the U.S. Navy in 1942 to produce them. They later applied the same molded plywood technology to aircraft parts. The Eameses became heads of the molded plywood division for Evans Products, though they retained their studio in Venice, California, throughout their career. The experimentation of the war years, the resulting improvements in technique, and the transition to factory production all contributed to the later success of the Eameses' molded plywood furniture.

After the war, in 1946, Eames's work was again honored in an exhibition at MOMA, this time a prestigious one-man furniture show—the first of its kind. In the exhibition, designed by the Eameses, the molded Plywood Chair (Figure 34) was first publicly shown, along with a collection of tables, screens, cases, and additional seating. Before the show opened, the Eameses were about ready to "run away to the circus." But the exhibition created great interest. George Nelson took the president of the Herman Miller Company along to see it and persuaded him to mass-produce the furniture. At first Evans Products was contracted, under Eames's supervision, to manufacture the design; in 1947 Herman Miller took over the production as well as the marketing.

Eames used monies from the sale of the 1946 Plywood Chair to continue his research. His next design, the Shell Chair of 1949 (Figure 35), was also an organic, three-dimensional molded design. With this piece, he branched into a new material—plastic reinforced with fiberglass. In 1956 the Eameses' Lounge Chair (Figure 36) of laminated rosewood and leather further explored the original material, plywood. All these designs used shells of constant thickness; later designs used cast metal members as in the framework of the 1958 Aluminum Group (Figure 37), the 1960 Time-Life Chair, the 1962 Tandem Seating, and the 1969 Soft-Pad Seating Group.

Eames did not design in a vacuum. On the one hand, he benefited from exposure to the technological advances of his time. And then on the other, Eames confirmed that, in terms of furniture design, Alvar Aalto's work in two-dimensional molded plywood was his most immediate point of reference, along with the work of Breuer, Le Corbusier, and Mies. The softer and more natural interpretations of Scandinavian designers in general reached North America in the 1930s; the Swedish imports, and later Finnish designs such as Aalto's were well known and widely available.

Though Eames received his greatest recognition for furniture design, he also exercised his talents in other fields. Eames excelled in residential architecture, his most outstanding design being his own house, known for its transparency, use of industrial components, and visual lightweightness. Of his more than fifty films, the better-known ones include *Blacktop* (1952); *Bread* (1952), a close-up perspective of international breads which included a special technique that actually allowed the viewer to smell the breads; *Toccata for Toy Trains* (1957), which won many international film festival awards; *Information Machine* (1958), for IBM; several segments for the "Fabulous Fifties" for CBS Television (winning two Emmy awards); and *Powers of Ten* (1969 and 1978), a general-audience physics film. His exhibition design, which spanned the globe, included *Glimpses of U.S.A.* (1959), a twelve-minute show for the U.S. State Department to introduce an exhibit in Moscow, consisting of 2,200 still and moving pictures simultaneously projected on seven screens; *Mathematica, a world of numbers . . . and beyond,* an exhibition for IBM which first opened at the Los Angeles Museum of Science and Industry in 1961 and appeared later in Chicago and Seattle; the IBM Pavilion (in collaboration with the office of Eero Saarinen's successors) for the New York World's Fair (1964), which featured a 22-screen film on problem solving; and *The World of Franklin and Jefferson,* first seen in Paris, Warsaw, and London in 1975, in the United States in 1976, and in Mexico City in 1977. Eames's involvement in education was not limited to his exhibitions: He taught and lectured at many American colleges and universities—including Cranbrook Academy of Art, the University of Georgia, U.C.L.A., Berkeley, Yale, and M.I.T.— as well as in Europe and the Far East. In 1970–71 he held the Charles Eliot Norton chair of poetry at Harvard. In all of these activities, Eames repeatedly expressed his concerns through the art of verbal and visual communication.

Charles Eames died in St. Louis on August 21,

1978. During his entire career he was an enthusiastic, productive worker. Even at the time of his death, he was traveling to consult on several different projects in St. Louis. The majority of Eames's works were created specially for others or for himself; he never patented his designs. The success Eames achieved was not the goal of a striving, competitive designer, but the byproduct of an unostentatious, unselfish man's love for his work. The design world will miss his open, friendly smile, which appeared in professional journals for over three decades. Although most people knew of him as a furniture maker, he regarded all of his work as architecture, and was honored by the architectural community. In 1977 the Eames house received the American Institute of Architect's "twenty-five-year award"; and in London in 1979, Ray Eames accepted the Queen's Gold Medal for Architecture on behalf of the Eames partnership. Undoubtedly her husband's name should go down in history as Charles Eames—creator.

Plywood Chair

Charles Eames's 1946 Plywood Chair evolved from the winning entry in the Museum of Modern Art's Organic Furniture Competition, organized in 1940 and exhibited in 1941. Eames had collaborated in the design with Eero Saarinen; Ray Kaiser worked on the presentation. Their entry introduced two technical advantages never before applied to furniture: three-dimensional molded plywood and an innovative procedure for bonding metal to a wooden shell with a rubber weld joint.

FIGURE 34
The Plywood Chair

Once Charles and Ray Eames moved to California, they devoted their evenings at home to improving the plywood molding technique. A stationary exercise bicycle provided the source of pressure needed to mold the plywood into a three-dimensional form. With heat and pressure being applied over large surfaces, danger was always present. (The myth that the apartment stove exploded during these experiments, however, should be laid to rest.) Later, they moved their equipment to a large garage in Venice, California, where in November 1942 they began work on a commission from the U.S. Navy for 5,000 molded plywood leg splints. With a group of young collaborators, (a sculptor, Marion Overby; an engineer-architect, Gregory Ain; a theatrical designer, Margaret Harris; and an architect, Griswald Raetze) they delivered the splints in three months.

Through the commission Colonel E. S. Evans, of Evans Products, learned of Eames's work, and in June 1943 he invited Charles and Ray to work for him. This offer afforded Eames the opportunity for more intense experimentation and improvement on the plywood molding and rubber joining techniques for furniture applications. Eames applied his findings to various pieces of furniture; this research led to the 1945 plywood furniture exhibited in the Museum of Modern Art one-man show in 1946.

With extreme awareness of the technical, comfort, and aesthetic aspects of his work, Eames searched for perfection in every detail. He kept abreast of the most up-to-date technical developments by collaborating closely with factory technicians. He preferred to develop the general configuration of a proposed chair from rough sketches and notes. Prototypes were developed using full-scale templates, which facilitated testing, rather than from technical drawings. Eames also employed many experimental sitters of various sizes, shapes, and contours. This testing assured that the final collection of templates forming the metal molds for mass production would provide comfort to a cross section of the population. Eames called these molding machines which he designed "KZAM!"s, the magician's word for a sudden transformation.

Moreover, Eames worked diligently to assure that the various elements—back, seat, and support—resulted in a look of unity. The elegance of the seat and back can be attributed to the relationship of their contours, which was complemented by the subtle curved lines of the steel frame.

The seat and back of the chair were composed of molded, five-layer, 6.5-mm ($\frac{5}{16}$") walnut plywood finished with melamine (a special finish applied during the molding process to provide a durable, scratch-resistant surface). The legs were formed by two inverted U-shaped rods, the front higher than the back, bent from 13.5-mm ($\frac{5}{8}$") solid chrome-plated steel. Connecting these with a special flattened weld, and carrying the back rest, was a spine of 7.0-mm ($^7/_{16}$″) solid chrome-plated steel. For resiliency, rubber shock mounts were bolted to the metal frame and electronically bonded to the wood, forming a flexible connection. The chair was shipped KD (knocked down) and assembled on site.

Eames produced two sizes of the chair. A lounge version measured 565 mm (22¼″) wide, 644 mm (25⅜″) deep, and 696 mm (27⅜″) high, with a seat height of 390 mm (15¼″). The dining chair version measured 495 mm (19½″) wide, 547 mm (21½″) deep, and 750 mm (29⅜″) high, with a seat height of 457 mm (18″).

During the years of experimentation in the 1940s the chair's shape and wood and the configuration of its legs varied frequently. There were natural walnut, ash, birch, and rosewood veneers. Birch was also available stained red, blue, yellow, or black. Upholstery bonded over foam latex onto the seat and back offered padded versions. Fabric and pony skin examples were shown in the 1946 MOMA one-man show. Variations of the legs included three-legged versions—either two legs in front and one in back, or the reverse. Another variation, which was discontinued, used laminated wooden legs and spine, slightly thicker than the

seat and back, and the same shock-mount connectors. The tilt-back version, still another variation, was a playful attempt at a chair which could be shifted forward or backward in two sitting positions.

Self-leveling nylon glides now replace the original rubber tips. Today only the four-legged version in natural veneers is available, in the original two sizes.

By means of new technical developments, which he helped to perfect, Eames directed post-World War II American furniture design toward a new consciousness of the industrial arts. His Plywood Chair was the mass-produced, durable, and versatile answer to the needs of the smaller, more economical, postwar American home.

Plastic Shell Chair

In 1948 the Eameses won second prize in the Museum of Modern Art's International Low-Cost Furniture Competition. Their entry, a stamped metal shell chair, was the forerunner of the 1949 fiberglass-reinforced polyester (FRP) Shell Chair. (Fiberglass was not available at the time of the competition.)

Eames conceived the shell structure before he decided what material to use for it. His design, which consolidated seat, back, and arms into one surface, was a refinement of the 1940 Organic Chair, also a shell design. As with his plywood designs, technical advancement during the war contributed to its realization. Eames was first introduced to fiberglass-reinforced plastic as a revolutionary, lightweight, durable material being used in the nosecones of British Mosquito Bombers. In 1948, Zenith Plastics was producing radar domes of fiberglass-reinforced plastic. While the Eames house was in the design phase, Eames learned of this source for the material. Recognizing its good features, he proposed to adapt it for mass-produced furniture. But at the time, mass production in this material was nonexistent; even the radar domes required custom handcrafting. Though he considered fiberglass-reinforced plastic and even aluminum, Eames eventually settled on sheet metal as the material for the 1948 competition entry.

Sheet metal satisfied Eames's prerequisites of economy and durability. And though the coldness of sheet metal necessitated a plastic coating, metal shells could be readily mass-produced by stamping, as in the automobile industry. Don Albinson even constructed a drop hammer in the Eameses' Venice, California, workshop for experimentation. With it, the competition entries were produced.

On November 28, 1948, the MOMA jury (consisting of seven members, including Mies van der Rohe and Catherine Bauer) awarded the Eames Shell Chair joint second prize.

In the following year an economical system evolved for manufacturing the Shell Chair in plastic: Fiberglass fibers were embedded in a matrix of polyester. In plastic, the design was lighter. It was also more durable; it resisted bending and denting. And it had the advantage of being naturally warmer to the touch without any additional coating.

But the changeover did cause some technical problems. Airborne glass particles were hazardous to factory workers. These particles also protruded through the surface so that hand sanding was required. Solutions to these problems were found during the first year of production, resulting in a marketable product.

The 1949 chair's shell was molded with a hydraulic press into its final three-dimensional form. The arm chair version was the first to be produced; the side chair followed in 1950. As with the metal competition entry, the plastic versions could be fitted with a variety of legs: rocker, four-legged, pedestal, or wire strut. The legs were attached with Eames's rubber shock mounts bonded to the fiberglass with epoxy, producing more resiliency than was inherent in the fiberglass alone. The original muted colors were indicative of the time: off-white, light and medium gray, and dark blue-gray. The color was unaffected by scratches or fading; it was

FIGURE 35
The Plastic Shell Chair

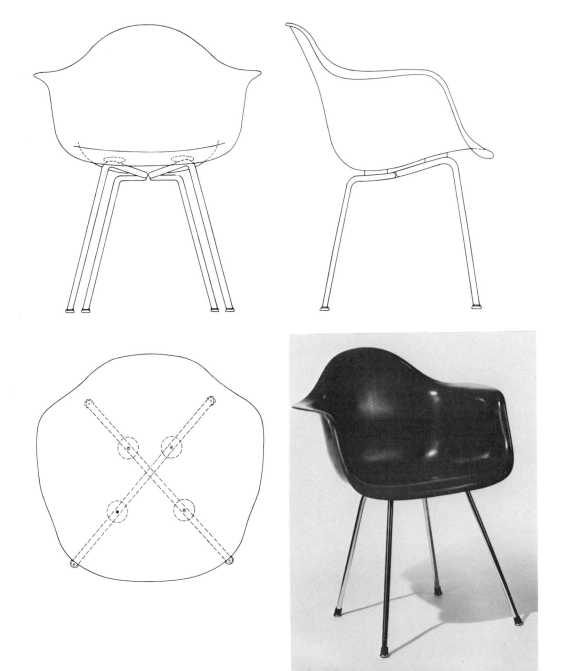

added into the liquid plastic before molding and became an integral part of the chair.

The measurements of the arm chair were 630 mm (24½") wide, 560 mm (22") deep, and 820 mm (32¼") high, with a seat height of 470 mm (18½"). The side chair measured 470 mm (18½") wide, 560 mm (22") deep, and 820 mm (32¼") high, with a seat height of 470 mm (18½").

Through the continuum of design that characterized Eames's practice, the shell chair was updated and improved over the years. In 1953, upholstery and padding were available on the shells. The 1954 stackable side chairs answered the need for flexible group seating. In 1963, tandem and auditorium seating were introduced. Today, the shell design is available with fabric or vinyl upholstery, with protective vinyl edges. In addition to the original arm and side chair versions, an extra-large arm chair has been added to the collection.

Of the original bases, only the four-legged and pedestal versions remain in production, but they have been exploited to the fullest extent.

Available, for example, are a wall-guarding four-legged version which prevents the upper edge of the chair from scratching the wall; ganging chair legs which enable the shells to be used separately or linked together with side clips to form long stable rows; and pedestals which swivel, tilt and swivel, or swivel and adjust in height. Color selections today include both naturals and brilliants. These almost endless variations enable the Shell Chairs to fulfill a wide range of needs.

Eames Lounge Chair and Ottoman

The Eames Lounge Chair and Ottoman, designed in 1955–1956, reflected Charles Eames's awareness of tradition as well as his way of approaching a problem. For comfort, he rediscovered traditional upholstery components: down and feather-filled cushions and luxurious leather. For greater resilience, he incorporated the rubber shock mounts invented for the

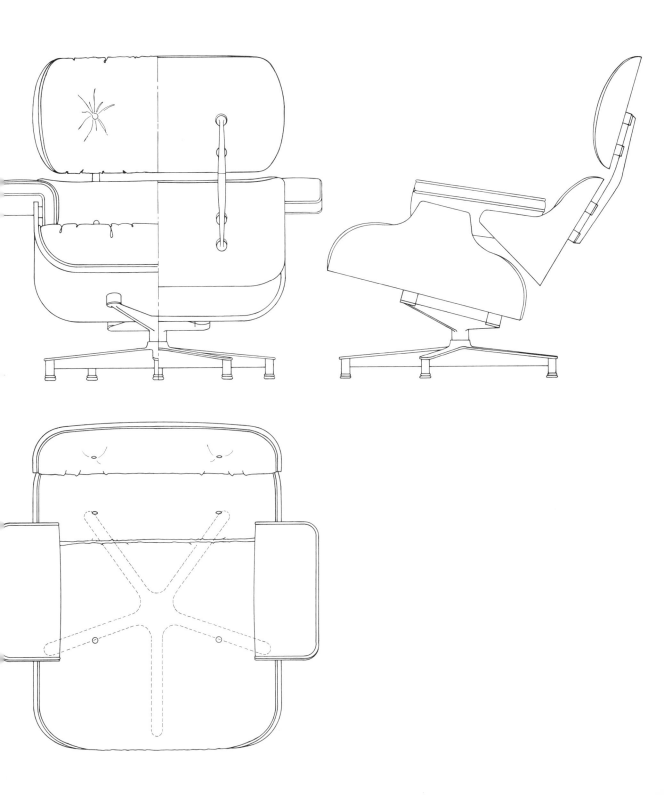

FIGURE 36

The Eames Lounge Chair and Ottoman

plywood chair. The chair is made up of three separate leather cushions, each with a curved plywood back, shock-mounted to clearly visible connecting elements. This separation of parts (reminiscent of the construction principle of the Plywood Chair) made it possible for the first time to mass-produce a chair as soft and deep as the English "club chair." Eames's sensitive uniting of old and new idioms made his lounge a chair of resounding beauty and comfort, one of the most popular designs of the twentieth century.

The lounge chair was supported on a pedestal with a five-prong base. One molded shell, one cushion, and a four-prong base composed the ottoman. The shells were cut from a single sheet of five-ply selected rosewood veneer plywood and formed in a hot-press metal die. The five inner plies were exposed on the edges. After sanding, the shells were hand-rubbed with wax. A leather covering zipped to a vulcanized fiber back formed each cushion; snaps secured the fiber backs to the plywood shells. Buttons of the same leather regulated the tufting. Two sizes of cushions were used: one for the two back shells, and one for the ottoman and the seat of the chair. These two cushion sizes differed not only in their shape but also in the down- and feather-filled envelope: The seat cushion incorporated a foam rubber block not found in the back. Twelve-gauge steel plates were bonded with foam rubber pads and upholstered with matching leather for the arms. Resilient neoprene shock mounts further cushioned the chair. Polished upper surfaces and flat-black baked enamel sides distinguished the cast aluminum base. Rubber cushioned the stainless steel glides.

The dimensions of the chair were 825 mm (32½") wide, 830 mm (32¾") deep, and 847 mm (33⅜") high, with a seat height of 380 mm (15"). The ottoman measured 660 mm (26") wide, 533 mm (21") deep, and 380 mm (15") high, with a seat height of 380 mm (15").

The appearance of the chair has remained basically the same through the years. However, a few minor changes have been made in the production equipment, the filling for the cushions, and the choice of leather.

In their size, weight, and obvious comfort, the Eames Lounge Chair and Ottoman were a departure from Eames's earlier designs, though the care and attention to detail remained consistent. This combination succeeded overwhelmingly. It offered the consumer a chair which complemented the contemporary environment and at the same time provided old-fashioned comfort.

Aluminum Group

Eames's first use of aluminum dated back to the MOMA Organic Furniture Competition of 1940, when aluminum was specified for the entry's legs because of its lightness and weather resistance. The Aluminum Group of 1958 began as a project for indoor-outdoor chairs. Like the Eames Lounge Chair of 1956, the chairs of the Aluminum Group were more costly than the Eames designs of the 1940s. But new production techniques also made possible some new forms. Slender aluminum members, varying in section, could now be reliably die-cast, with surfaces that would take a fine polish.

In the Aluminum Group, in contrast to the Plywood and fiberglass Shell Chairs, a metal

FIGURE 37
The Aluminum Chair

framework (on a pedestal base) held in tension a thin pad of heat-sealed upholstery which forms the seat and back. Ingeniously simple, lighter, and more mobile than the Eames Lounge Chair, the Aluminum Group with its multifunctional bases surpassed earlier chairs in versatility.

Eames designed three chair types for varied activities: a low-back and a high-back desk chair, each with an inward curve to support the lower back for upright active sitting, and a high-back lounge chair with a headrest and a matching ottoman. This lounge contained a relaxing concave back reminiscent of Eames's earlier lounge (Figure 36). Loop-shaped arms of molded aluminum could be connected to the side frame. Slight variations occurred in the group according to functional requirements, but all three had the same structural principles.

The most innovative element of the design was its layered pad, in which three materials were fused into a sturdy, stable sling upholstery. The inner layer consisted of a 6.3-mm (¼") vinyl foam pad, which provided bulk and softness. This padding was sandwiched by vinyl-coated nylon fabric, vinyl, or leather. High-frequency currents and pressure fused these five layers together in lines 50 mm (1⅞") apart, producing a horizontally ribbed surface.

The sling seat was formed by securing the pad to the chair's side frame. Cast in one piece, each side consisted of a supporting flanged bar with short horizontal cylindrical extensions on each end. The edge of the upholstery pad was inserted over the flange and anchored with screws. At top and bottom, the edge of the pad was rolled, and was held at each end by wrapping around the two small cylinders at the ends of the side bars. This method of attaching the upholstery to the frame eliminated the need for rigid support at the top and bottom of the seat, making sitting more comfortable.

To hold the pad in tension, two U-shaped aluminum braces, arched away from the sling, connected the side frames. One brace was located at the upper back; the other was under the seat and provided the point of attachment to the pedestal base. A vertical stem of black enameled steel mounted the chair on its four-prong base. Selected for its strength, this stem was the only major element not of cast aluminum. Bases which tilted, adjusted in height, and swiveled were available with or without casters.

The low chair of the group measured 533 mm (21") wide, 590 mm (23¼") deep, and 850 mm (33½") high, with a seat height of 470 mm

(18½"). The high-back chair measured 575 mm (22½") wide, 585 mm (23") deep, and 1,003 mm (39½") high, with a seat height of 420 mm to 470 mm (16½" to 18½"). The lounge chair measured 560 mm (22") wide, 725 mm (28½") deep, and 860 mm (33¾") high, with a seat height of 445 mm (17½"). The reclining chair measured 585 mm (23") wide, 795 mm (31¼") deep, and 1,003 mm (39½") high, with a seat height of 406 mm (16"). The ottoman measured 545 mm (21¼") wide, 540 mm (21⅛") deep and 457 mm (18") high, with a seat height of 457 mm (18").

The original aluminum design served as a functional starting point for other designs. In 1967 the base was replaced by the four-prong "universal" base, used from then on for all of Eames's pedestal chairs except the lounge chair. Continual revision refined the tilt and swivel mechanisms. The molded Aluminum

Chair framework and upholstery technique remained the same, but the upholstery was modified in the 1969 Soft-Pad Group, in which leather-covered polyurethane foam cushions were attached to the sling pad to enhance the comfort of the original group.

The technical advances and streamlined appearance of the Eames Aluminum Group emerged as the world was beginning its heavy concentration on space exploration. Perhaps as no other furniture, the Aluminum Group captured this pioneering—and at the same time futuristic—spirit.

Eero Saarinen

The architect Eero Saarinen played an important role in the history of furniture design. Before him, other designers such as Mies and Le Corbusier had concentrated heavily on revolutionizing materials and construction techniques. Saarinen, however, gave a new definition to the twentieth-century chair "look": He augmented earlier considerations by concentrating on innovating form as well. The furniture resulting from his approach was a sophisticated sculptural foretaste of the rebellious designs which evolved in the 1960s.

Saarinen was born on August 20, 1910, in Kirkkonummi, Finland. His home environment unquestionably influenced and stimulated his furniture and architectural careers. His father was the internationally known architect Eliel Saarinen (1873–1950). Loja Gesellus, Saarinen's mother, was a sculptor, weaver, architectural modelmaker, and photographer. Under their guidance, the ambidextrous young Saarinen experimented in painting and drawing in the 90-foot studio of the family's home/studio complex. Located 50 kilometers from Helsinki on Lake Hvittrask, the Saarinen residence was a refuge for creative energy and thought. Saarinen and his older sister Pipsan spent many

inspirational hours in the company of such notables as Carl Milles, the Swedish sculptor; Julius Mier-Fraefe, the German critic; Gustav Mahler, the Austrian composer; and Jean Sibelius, the Finnish composer.

Not only did Eliel Saarinen direct his son's life into architecture, he also instilled in him his own lifelong competitive spirit. Encouraged to enter competitions, the 12-year-old Eero Saarinen won first place in a Swedish matchstick design contest. (Though during an unlucky streak in college he became known as "Second-Place Saarinen," he was normally very successful with his competition entries throughout his life.) In the following year, 1923, his father placed second in the international competition for the new *Chicago Tribune* building, and used the $20,000 prize money to move his family to America.

As it had in Finland, the Saarinen's home in the United States generated excitement and encouraged creativity. After brief stays in Evanston, Illinois, and Ann Arbor, Michigan, the family settled permanently in Bloomfield Hills, Michigan, in 1925. Eliel Saarinen accepted the presidency of the newly established Cranbrook Academy of Art, which under his pioneering guidance became an outstanding center of design education. He was also awarded the commission to design forty buildings of the Cranbrook Complex. This commission involved the entire family: Saarinen's mother designed tapestries, draperies, and upholstery for the Art Deco Kingswood School for Girls; Pipsan decorated the dining hall; and Eero executed his first furniture—bold, sculptural wooden chairs.

This sculptural tendency, seen in all Saarinen's furniture and attributable to his mother's influence, was so intense that in 1929 he went to Paris and pursued sculpture at the Académie de la Grand Chaumière for one year. In 1930, however, he returned to the United States and to his father's career. Although he was foremost an architect for the remainder of his life, all aspects of his later work were affected by his concern for three-dimensional design.

When Saarinen returned to the United States, he worked for four weeks in the architectural office of Norman Bel Geddes in New York City before enrolling in Yale's School of Architecture. Excelling in the Beaux Arts styled program, he received the Charles O. Matcham Traveling Fellowship upon his graduation in 1934. With the fellowship he returned to Europe for two years. The first year he spent traveling and observing both the architecture of the past and the progressive designs of the Modern movement. During the second, he worked in the architectural office of Jarl Eklund in Helsinki, Finland. When he returned to Bloomfield Hills in 1936, he entered into a partnership with his father and joined the architectural teaching staff at Cranbrook.

His professional years in Bloomfield Hills provided additional growth for Saarinen. His father's architecture became more clearly defined, and eventually influenced Saarinen's own philosophy in such principles as the integrity of the building on its site and the incorporation of surprise elements. As a teacher at Cranbrook, Saarinen made invaluable contact with many talented people: Harry Bertoia, Harry Weese, Ralph Rapson, and Florence Schust (later Knoll). But most important, at least in relation to his furniture career, Saarinen began a longstanding friendship with the architect and furniture designer Charles Eames.

In 1940 Saarinen and Eames combined their backgrounds and ingenuity to design the winner of the 1940–1941 Museum of Modern Art Organic Furniture Competition. Their goal was to design a chair of "organic" form in which all parts blended into a single unit using a single material. This approach to form modernized the traditional chair. Saarinen and Eames's revolutionary new material, three-dimensional molded plywood, made possible the formation of seat, back, and arms in one consolidated shell: Form followed material!

A nagging problem, however, remained: the dissociation of the legs from the body of the chair. This issue plagued Saarinen and countless other furniture designers throughout the 1940s. In Saarinen's quest to design a truly organic chair, his Womb Chair (Figure 38) of 1946 was a compromise. But finally, in 1957, visual unity was achieved in Saarinen's Pedestal Group.

Saarinen believed not only that a chair should be unified as an object, but that it should coexist in unity with its user and its architectural setting. To Saarinen, the chair was not complete until somebody sat in it. He continually strove to design furniture that was complete when used and that in turn complemented the user. Since his chairs were meant for a wide range of people, he designed them to suit the average person. Likewise, he considered his chairs' relation to architecture in terms of their proportion and scale to the floors, walls, ceilings, and overall space. This concern for unity was also the basis of his architectural fame.

When his father died in 1950, Eero Saarinen continued the twenty-five-year-old architectural office, though he redirected it away from his father's traditional tendencies. This independence in design philosophy had surfaced two years earlier when the Saarinens separately entered the competition for the Jefferson Westward Expansion Memorial in St. Louis—which Eero Saarinen won! As Eero Saarinen and Associates, the firm expanded through the 1950s and became one of the most sought-after architectural firms in the country.

Saarinen's outstanding architectural contributions include the Jefferson Westward Expansion Memorial in St. Louis, Missouri (1948–1964); the General Motors Technical Center in Warren, Michigan (1948–1956); the Kresge Auditorium and the Chapel at M.I.T. in Boston, Massachusetts (1953–1955); the United States Embassy in London (1955–1961); the United States Embassy in Oslo (1959); the Dulles International Airport near Chantilly, Virginia (1961); the Trans World Airline Terminal at Kennedy International Airport in New York City (1956–1962); and the CBS Building, also in New York City (1962–1964). Saarinen's architecture had no unified style. While reflecting the established concepts of the Modern movement, his *responsible architecture* also expressed the individuality of each project.

Eero Saarinen was a diligent designer. He loved his work and worked hard at it, often late into the night. He was meticulous, making hundreds of sketches and many models to refine details. He pioneered many new materials and construction techniques. Proud of his design process, he stipulated in his will that no building or project could carry his name unless he himself had worked on it.

Eero Saarinen died on September 1, 1961, after undergoing brain surgery for the removal of a tumor. His untimely death brought to an end the life of an easy-mannered, competitive, intense giant of architecture and furniture design.

Womb Chair

In 1946 Eero Saarinen designed one of the most comfortable Contemporary chairs ever made—the Womb Chair. Like all of Saarinen's work, the Womb Chair resulted from an analysis of a specific human need for comfort and an awareness of the aesthetic qualities that met the contemporary needs of humanity.

The design of the Womb Chair resulted from two considerations. First, Saarinen was interested in comfort. He sought a replacement for the traditional overstuffed Victorian lounge chair so common in American homes. Realizing that the modern sitter had a tendency to slump (something a proper Victorian would never have done!) and was not content to remain in any one position for long, he designed a chair that conformed to such sitting habits. Second, Saarinen sought a chair that would unify interior space and architecture. His Womb Chair met both these needs perfectly—its ample scale related to his architecture and yet accommodated its user.

The chair was very wide and very deep, but had a thin profile. A molded plastic shell was padded with an upholstery-covered doughnut-shaped cushion of latex foam. Two separate round latex foam cushions provided additional comfort in the shell. The entire chair was supported on its four legs and the skeletal framework—both of bent rod steel.

The measurements of the chair were: 1,016 mm (40") wide, 865 mm (34") deep, and 900 mm (35½") high, with a seat height of 406 mm (16") and an arm height of 520 mm (20½").

Not only was Saarinen's concern for comfort one of the initial factors in the chair's conception; it also served as the inspiration for the chair's name. When sitting in the chair, one comfortably and almost automatically assumed a fetal position—whence the name "Womb Chair." Hans Knoll (1914–1955), then director of Knoll Associates, the manufacturer of the chair, asked Saarinen to suggest an alternate name. Saarinen replied, "I have been thinking and thinking about a printable name for that chair, but my mind keeps turning to those which are more biological rather than less biological." The name stuck.

The Womb Chair prompted other pieces of furniture that Saarinen introduced at the same time. For additional comfort, he designed an ottoman to complement the chair. He also extended the width of the chair and thus formed a sofa. But of this collection, the Womb Chair remained the most comfortable piece of furniture for relaxed sitting.

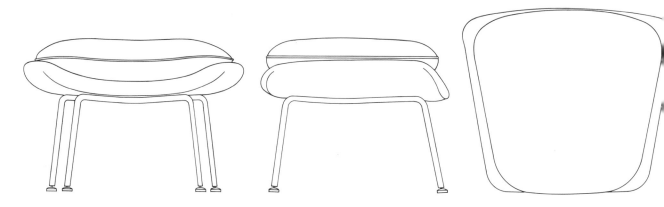

FIGURE 38
The Womb Chair

Pedestal Group

Eero Saarinen's 1957 Pedestal Group of Furniture resulted from his search for furniture that would unclutter interiors of their usual jumble of legs. In achieving this goal, he also arrived at furniture with an organically unified form—a form he had sought throughout his entire furniture career.

The Pedestal Group consisted of an armchair (Figure 39), a side chair (Figure 40), two stools (Figure 41), and a series of tables (Figure 42).

The chairs were of three parts: a cast aluminum base with plastic coating matching the color of the metal, a molded plastic shell reinforced with fiberglass, and an upholstered pad of latex foam. The upholstery was zippered over the foam rubber pad, and the pad was secured to the steel by Velcro. The arm chair measured 660 mm (26") wide, 597 mm (23½") deep, and 812 mm (32") high, with a seat height of 470 mm (18½") and an arm height of 645 mm (25⅜"). The side chair measured 495 mm (19½") wide, 560 mm (22") deep, and 825 mm (32½") high, with a 470-mm (18½") seat height.

The two stools were identical in form except for height. Their bases were the same cast aluminum as that of the chairs. An upholstered latex foam pad which formed the seat was permanently secured to the base. A swiveling mechanism was available upon order. The taller stool measured 380 mm (15") in diameter and 450 mm (17⅝") high, while the shorter measured 380 mm (15") in diameter and 406 mm (16") high.

The tables, which, like the stools, used the same base as the chairs, varied in size and choice of tops. They ranged in height—390 mm

(15¼"), 520 mm (20½"), 660 mm (26"), and 725 mm (28½"). The tops were available in a number of sizes and two different shapes, round and oval.

Frequent changes have occurred in the finishes and materials of the Pedestal Group. In 1957, when the furniture was first marketed, it was available in four colors: white, charcoal, gray (almost beige), and a "special" black. By 1962, the standard colors became white and beige (the gray renamed). Beige joined black as a "special" in 1973–1974, leaving only white as the standard color. The table tops have always been available in a variety of materials and finishes: Italian Cremo marble; colored marble, including gray beige, brown rose, and dark brown; white plastic laminate; and various wood veneers, including oak with a lacquer finish, mahogany with a satin finish, and walnut with an oiled finish.

In designing the group, Saarinen made hundreds of sketches and studies on paper. Quarter-size models were then made to refine the form's lines and proportions. Eventually, full-size prototypes were constructed, which Saarinen tested on his family and friends in his own home in Bloomfield Hills.

Collaborating with Don Petit and the Knoll Design Research Team, Saarinen determined that to make the chair *technically* "organic" was not possible. The base had to be made of cast aluminum in order to support the chair, and thus the oneness of materials needed for the chair to be fully organic was not possible. Saarinen was disappointed. Until his death, he continued to search for the technique and/or material needed to make his chair completely

FIGURE 39
The Saarinen Pedestal Arm Chair

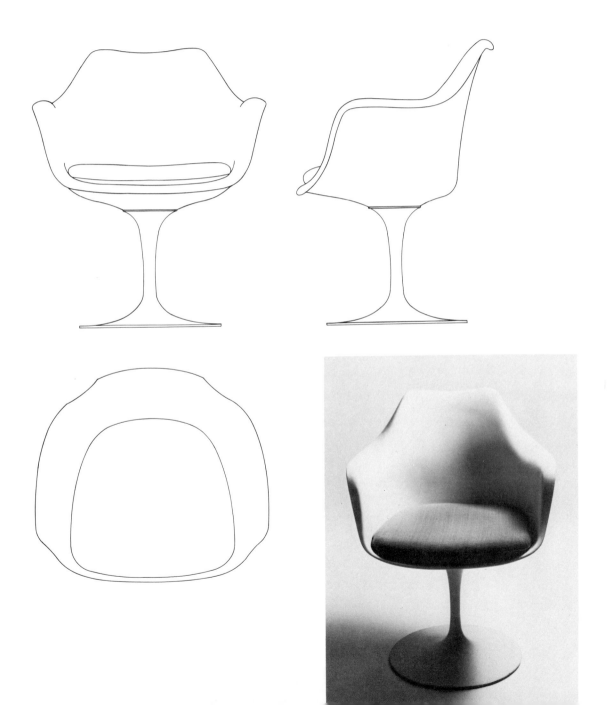

organic. Though plastics exist today that would allow the chair to be constructed solely of one material, the finishes available are not of the quality required. Once this problem is solved, the chair can be manufactured as originally designed. Even though Saarinen had to compromise in the organic nature of the material, his organic form met with immediate success.

To understand completely the success and impact of the Saarinen Pedestal Group, one has only to note the hundreds of copies it inspired. None of these copies, however, succeeded in matching the original group's graceful unity, so carefully achieved by Eero Saarinen.

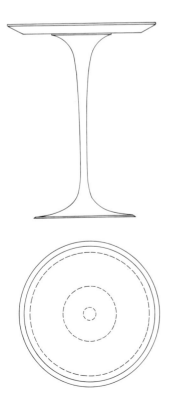

The 1960s and 1970s: A Potpourri of Design

The hodgepodge decades of the sixties and seventies contained facets of every previous design tendency and were fully endowed with their own creative spirit as well. They began calmly enough with lingerings of the' serene sparseness of the "Minimal Style." But after a decade of conservative reworkings of the earlier Rational concepts, the design world exploded into tangents as dynamic and full of individual color as ever witnessed in twentieth-century design.

Though a wealth of conventional designs was presented, the distinction of the period was found in the imaginations of the iconoclasts. Eero Saarinen opened the door, giving new unity to traditional chair and table forms with his revolutionary supports. Now furniture parts and materials were able to be reduced into one single state—both an economical advantage as well as a stimulus to the imagination. The very essence of tables, chairs, and beds, as well as their social impact, was called into question by the relaxed life-styles, new standards of comfort, and open-mindedness of the rebellious young adults of the postwar "baby boom." As in the political and social orders, newcomers on the international design scene questioned the cherished, long-established concepts as to what furniture consisted of and what functions it fulfilled.

In any design era, it is materials and construction techniques as well as life-styles that set the bounds and make the rules for designers. In this respect the 1960s and 1970s were richly endowed with means for creativity. All previous materials, from tubular steel to molded plywood, were at the disposal of designers. In their attempts to simplify design and reduce costs, some designers really got down to basics—air, water, and in the case of the design group of Gatti, Paolini, and Teodoro, plastic "beans." But the most fertile substances during the late sixties and early seventies became the growing family of plastics. Not only was a wide variety of forms available, such as clear and opaque rigid structures and soft films and foams of various densities, but the methods of working the materials also far surpassed the original techniques of earlier decades. In addition to compression molding, blow, vacuum, and injection molding could economically form shells, ribbons, and foam blocks. Conformists as well as nonconformists took advantage of the economy of construction and wide range of design possibilities of plastics.

Due to the oil crisis of the 1970s, the plastics boom lost its momentum. Molded plywood and laminated wood, almost forgotten materials, started receiving serious attention once again. And though a single material might have been preferred for a time, no exclusive substance, such as steel during the 1920s, completely captivated international design during this period.

Eclecticism is the best overall descriptive term for the designs of recent years. Interior designers and architects freely mixed shapes and materials. Breuer's Bauhaus furniture was presented next to "Pop" designs, primitive art juxtaposed with ultramodern, amorphous form accompanied rigid geometrics. But more dramatic than these couplings was the nonexistence of concise movements and previous regional characteristics, due mostly to stepped-up communication within the design world. For example, during the mid-sixties Scandinavian designers, known for decades for their natural wood designs, excelled in plastics, as was seen in the work of Eero Aarnio and Verner Panton. (Panton's side chair accomplished what Saarinen had attempted with his pedestal furniture: It was the first solid-plastic design manufactured.) Meanwhile many northern European designers rediscovered wood, Italians introduced all-polyurethane foam furniture, and in America Warren Platner created sculptural furniture from metal rods, while Richard Schultz experimented in thin polyester fabric in his elegant aluminum outdoor furniture. As for form, only the designers themselves outnumbered the sundry directions taken.

Since recent Contemporary designs have so far defied conventional cataloging, decades are best broken down into their short-lived, overlapping movements. International trends are rarely found. The general tendency at the beginning of the 1960s, in addition to Miesian art, was to review and expand on previous forms. Pedestals, shell constructions, and cantilevers abounded. Then slowly, with the increased use of thick foam upholstery and molded plastic, the rigid contours and regular forms of the previous decade gave way to soft, rounded edges and fancy shapes—some with Art Nouveau flavor. Designs by Olivier Mourgue, Jørn Utzon, and Pierre Paulin at times featured these characteristics. Upholstery padding continued to grow until by the end of the decade it had replaced legs on sofas and chairs altogether. Excellent examples of this revolutionary, resilient, single-component furniture were given by Cini Boeri and Sebastian Matta. Both men were designing in Italy, which—if credit goes to any region for spearheading innovation—was at the top of the list in both research and creativity.

From the mid-sixties Italian design began to attract more and more international attention. By the turn of the decade, annual visitors to international furniture fairs were scurrying past other exhibition halls to find out what the Italians had recently been up to. Then in 1972 their "New Domestic Landscape" was featured at the Museum of Modern Art in New York. True to the era, however, the Italians presented a variety of interpretations of their new concepts for interior furnishings.

The serious works of Gae Aulenti, Tobia and Afra Scarpa, Vico Magistretti, and Achille and Pier Castiglioni displayed new materials at their sophisticated best. The designs of Joe Colombo promoted a radically original idea—modular furniture systems. In many of his systems individual pieces of furniture as well as their positional grouping afforded endless opportunities for personalized interiors. Then to the extreme left (considered by many to be insubordination!) were the furniture curiosities, such as those by the design groups of Studio 65 and de Pas/d'Urbino/Lomazzi. When one perched on their comfortable ionic capitals, baseball gloves, and lips, the message rang clear: Furniture design need not always be such a ponderous subject.

With the advent of the "Me Generation" in the 1970s, the pendulum again swung to boxy shapes, with legs, if any, flush to the design's edges. But this time, instead of the austere finishes of the International Style, basic shapes were frequently decked with an almost Art Deco opulence. With the attitude of "Why should I design in stainless steel when my clients can afford gold plate?", materials could be anything but economical. Simultaneous with these luxurious tendencies, however, designers such as Rodney Kinsman and the young design team of Morrison and Hannah continued to provide lower-priced markets with well-designed, practical furnishings.

Most of the designers listed so far are still in the prime of their design careers. But theirs have not been the only designs on the market.

All the while, the 1920s classics have continued to be the hallowed firsts of the Contemporary design community, and now they are also well known to the design-conscious public. Each year new designs and variations of color and material are introduced, many of which are being mass-produced for the first time since their designing in the 1920s and 1930s. With the "Whole Earth" outlook of the early 1970s, the natural beauty of Scandinavian masterpieces has also made a comeback. The works of Eames and Saarinen, of course, have never faded from the showroom floors. And after 100 years, Thonet's work still has that avant-garde flair. So, in spite of the screams and shouts of the "Post-Modernists," Contemporary furniture, both established classics and recent additions, has never enjoyed more popularity.

The multiplicity of recent Contemporary furniture design should provide sufficient material for very interesting readings to come. For now, its overall impact and eventual course are not yet fully revealed. Considering the variety of evidence at hand, however, one point *is* clear. The ultimate winner of the Muthesius/van de Velde argument for and against uniformity in Modern design was certainly not Muthesius. The extent to which variety and individuality are valued in our age has not been better manifested than in the furniture designs it has produced.

Contemporary Design Movements and Their Influences

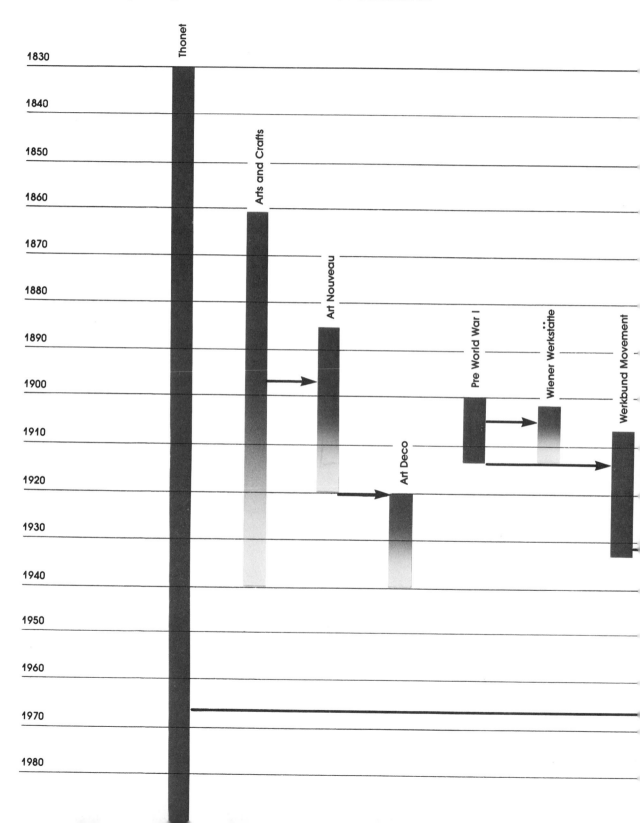

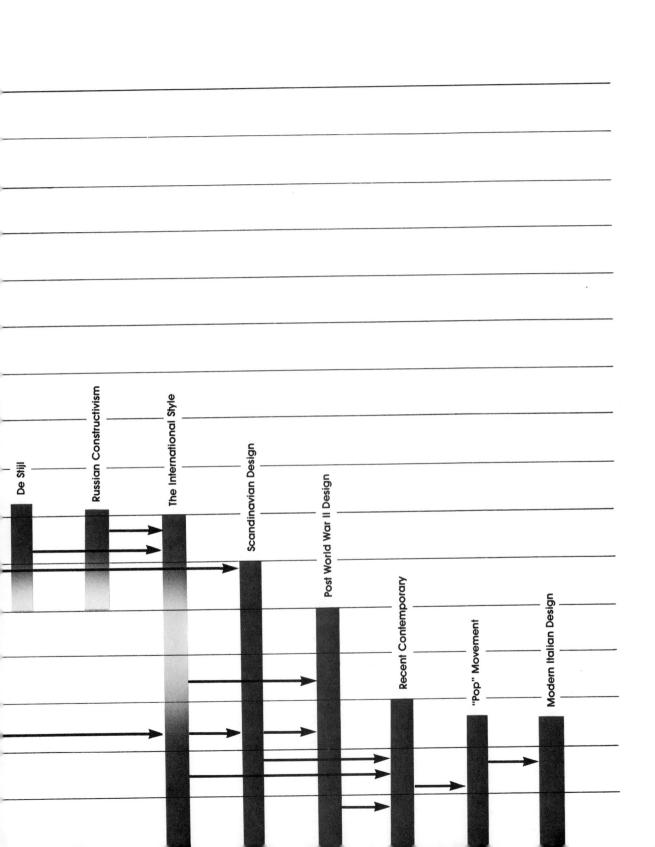

De Stijl

Russian Constructivism

The International Style

Scandinavian Design

Post World War II Design

Recent Contemporary

"Pop" Movement

Modern Italian Design

Michael Thonet

Michael Thonet	1796–1871	Austrian

Arts and Crafts

Ashbee, Charles	1863–1942	English
Burges, William	1827–1881	English
Morris, William	1834–1896	English
Vorsey, Charles F.A.	1857–1941	English

Art Nouveau

Endell, August	1871–1925	German
Galliard, Eugène	1862–1933	French
Gaudi i Cornet, Antoni	1852–1926	Spanish
Guimard, Hector	1867–1942	French
Hoffmann, Josef	1870–1956	Austrian
Horta, Victor	1861–1947	Belgian
Mackintosh, Charles Rennie	1868–1928	English
Mackmurdo, Arthur Heygate	1851–1942	English
Majorelle, Louis	1859–1926	English
Moser, Koloman	1868–1918	Austrian
Obrist, Hermann	1863–1927	German
Olbrich, Joseph	1867–1908	Austrian
Riemerschmid, Richard	1868–1957	German
Vallin, Eugène		French
van de Velde, Henry	1863–1957	Belgian

Werkbund Movement

Behrens, Peter	1868–1940	German
Gropius, Walter	1883–1969	German
Muthesius, Hermann	1861–1927	German
van de Velde, Henry	1863–1957	Belgian

De Stijl

Doesburg, Theo van	1883–1931	Dutch
Reitveld, Gerritt Thomas	1888–1964	Dutch

Russian Constructivism

Tatlin, Vladimir	1885–1953	Russian

The Rational International Style

Albers, Josef	1888–1976	German
Breuer, Marcel	1902–1981	Hungarian
Gropius, Walter	1883–1969	German
Le Corbusier	1887–1965	Swiss
Mies van der Rohe, Ludwig	1886–1969	German
Perriand, Charlotte	1903–	French
Reich, Lilly	1885–1947	German
Roth, Alfred	1903–	German
Stam, Mart	1899–	Dutch

Scandinavian

Aalto, Alvar	1898–1976	Finnish
Klint, Kaare	1888–1954	Danish
Juhl, Finn	1912–	Danish
Mathsson, Bruno	1907–	Swedish
Mogensen, Børge	1914–	Danish
Risom, Jens	1916–	Danish
Wegner, Hans J.	1914–	Danish

Post-World War II Design

Bassett, Florence Knoll	1917–	American
Bertoia, Harry	1915–1978	Italian
Eames, Charles	1907–1978	American
Haussmann, Robert	1931–	Swiss
Jacobsen, Arne	1902–1971	Danish
Kjaerholm, Poul	1929–1980	Danish
Knoll, Florence (see Bassett)		
Nelson, George	1907–1986	American
Saarinen, Eero	1910–1961	Finnish

Recent Contemporary Design

Harcourt, Geoffrey	1935–	English
Kinsman, Rodney		English
Morrison and Hannah		American
Mourgue, Olivier	1939–	French
Panton, Verner	1926–	Danish
Paulin, Pierre	1927–	French
Platner, Warren	1919–	American
Schultz, Richard	1926–	American

"Pop" Design

Aarnio, Eero	1932–	Danish
DePas/d'Urbino/Lomazzi	c. 1930s	Italian
Gatti/Paolini/Teodoro	c. 1940s	Italian
Studio 65		

Modern Italian

Aulenti, Gae	1927–	Italian
Boeri, Cini	1924–	Italian
Castiglioni, Achille	1918–	Italian
Castiglioni, Pier	1914–	Italian
Colombo, Joe	1930–1971	Italian
Magistretti, Vico	1920–	Italian
Matta, Sebastian		Brazilian
Scarpa, Afra	1937–	Italian
Scarpa, Tobia	1935–	Italian

Glossary

Aluminum A lightweight, whitish metal which is highly malleable and corrosion-resistant. To improve aluminum's durability, small amounts of silicon and iron are usually added. Though publicly introduced in the 1855 Paris Exhibition, aluminum was not commercially produced until the late nineteenth century. Its lightweightness was utilized by Marcel Breuer in his furniture of 1933 and as a frequent material in the postwar designs of Charles Eames.

Arc Any continuous segment of a circle or symmetrical bow shape. (See Barcelona Chair, Figure 11.)

Art Deco A decorative design movement named after the 1925 L'Exposition Internationale des Arts Decoratifs et Industriels Modernes in Paris and terminating in both Europe and America in the economic depression of the 1930s. Though frequently using modern materials and production techniques as did Bauhaus designers, Art Deco designers were antifunctional. Motifs of primitive cultures such as the Aztecs and Egyptians, geometric decoration, exotic materials, and vivid color characterized much of Art Deco design.

Art Nouveau An art movement of the late nineteenth and early twentieth centuries in Europe and America which strove to eliminate historical revivals from design. Nature was the inspiration of its decorative expression.

Arts and Crafts An English art movement inspired by William Morris which strove to upgrade nineteenth-century furniture by offering a sturdy alternative to industrial products. The philosophies of the movement remained strong in England, Scandinavian countries, and other areas of the Continent well into the twentieth century.

Bauhaus Although short-lived, the single most dominant force in directing the course of Contemporary design. The school was founded in 1919 by the German architect and designer Walter Gropius as an incorporation of the Art Academy and the School of Arts and Crafts of Weimar, Germany, which Henry van de Velde had previously headed. Constantly harassed by the growing Nazi Party, the school relocated in 1925 to Dessau, Germany, and in 1932 to Berlin. After Gropius resigned in 1928, the architect Hannes Meyer directed the Bauhaus until 1930; then Mies van de Rohe continued as head until its closing in 1933.

Beaux Arts (Fr) Literally, the fine arts. During the late nineteenth and early twentieth century, the term applied to art and architectural schools whose curriculum stressed the study and imitation of past design eras.

Bergère (Fr) An arm chair with completely upholstered seat, back, and arms.

Bolster A long cylindrical-shaped cushion to support the head; a pillow. (See Mies Couch, Figure 17, and Le Corbusier Chaise Longue, Figure 18.)

Buttoned A tufted upholstery feature in which buttons, frequently covered with the upholstery fabric, are sewn over the points of tufting as a finishment. (See Barcelona Chair, Figure 11).

Caning Slender pieces of bamboo, rattan, cane, or palm which are woven to form the seats and/or backs of furniture. (See Thonet's Design No. 14, Figure 1.)

Cantilever A twentieth-century structural detail, seen in both furniture and architectural design, in which a horizontal member projects beyond a vertical support, resulting in a light, floating effect. (See MR Chair, Figure 10.)

Canvas A stiff, durable, heavyweight fabric of plain woven cotton or linen frequently used for awnings, tents, and furniture upholstery.

Chaise Longue (Fr) Literally, a "long chair." A reclining chair with back and head rest at one end only. (See Le Corbusier's Chaise Longue, Figure 18.)

Chrome-plated steel Carbon steel which has been electroplated with chromium, a shiny white metal able to prevent the steel from corroding. The plating process was perfected in the United States in 1924. When introduced to the market the following year, chrome plating quickly replaced nickel in many areas of use because of chromium's brighter or more retentive color.

Conchoidal A three-dimensional form having both convex and concave contours; shell-like.

Cyma Recta Curve An S-shaped curve which begins and ends horizontally. (See Barcelona Chair, Figure 11; and Tugendhat Chair, Figure 13.)

Danish Cabinetmaker's Guild A professional association started in the late 1920s by a group of twenty-five master craftsmen. With increased competition from industrial products and the low state of the Danish economy, the guild was formed out of its members' concern for the future of the trade. To publicize their quality products, an annual exhibition was held in Copenhagen. Though at first only a local affair, the exhibition accelerated in size and influence to become a major international design event in the 1960s. Not only did the annual guild exhibitions preserve century-old values of Danish furniture design, but the interaction and competition of architects and designers introduced new furniture forms and construction methods to the traditional art of furniture making.

Dowel A round headless pin of wood or metal used to hold two adjacent parts together. A dowel is inserted into holes of corresponding size.

Enamel Finish A varnish composed of organic oils and gums which is baked onto a metal surface to produce a hard, durable opaque finish (not to be confused with glasslike porcelain enamel coatings). (See Le Corbusier's Basculant Chair, Figure 21.)

Expressionistic Design A popular German movement in both architecture and furniture design just prior to and after World War I, characterized by bold, representational forms. During the early 1920s Expressionism slowly lost ground to the strongly emerging Rational concept of design, which it directly opposed. However, many supporters and precursors of the Rational or International Style were briefly involved in Expressionism. Behrens, Gropius, Wright, and even Mies van der Rohe produced designs which suggested Expressionistic influences: a unique interpretation of a design project; impressive but functionally unnecessary detailing; a sense of plasticity—the characteristic which best generalizes the movement. Eric Mendelsohn was perhaps the best known of the principal Expressionistic designers.

Fiberglass-Reinforced Plastic (FRP) Plastic in which glass fibers or glass fabric have been incorporated during the molding process. The embedded glass adds to the strength and durability of the finished plastic product. (See Eames's Shell Chair, Figure 35.)

Finish In furniture, any material which protects or aesthetically complements a design. Generally, finishes can be classified as hard or soft, permanent or temporary. The oils used by Wegner emphasize the wood's beauty and warmth while preserving the material. But such light finishes are not as durable as, for instance, Le Corbusier's use of baked enamel, which also protects as well as providing aesthetic effect.

Flange A retaining edge or ridge projecting from an object's surface. (See arm support of Basculant Chair, Figure 21.)

Flat Bar Steel A solid piece of steel that is stronger and heavier than tubular steel. (See Brno Chair, Figure 14.)

Foam Rubber An expanded structure of either natural latex or synthetic rubber (polyurethane) formed by incorporating bubbles into the dope (the material's liquid state). When set, a foam block or sheet of high resiliency results. The foam's density as well as a number of additional physical properties can be varied, which explains its varied end uses. Natural latex foams were introduced in the early 1930s. Since World War II synthetic foams have been available which are more durable but do not recover as quickly from compression as the natural latex. In addition to padding for upholstery, foams have been utilized as a comprehensive furniture material since the mid 1960s.

Inlay A decorative design created by inserting contrasting materials into a surface of solid wood, stone, metal, etc. When complete, the design is embedded into the ground material, flush to its surface.

Joinery The art or trade of one who assembles wood constructions. Also, the connections which secure woodwork. Mortise-and-tenon, dowel, and dovetail are common means of jointing.

KD (Knocked Down) Describes furniture which can be shipped or stored disassembled as a flat package and quickly reassembled at its final destination.

Lacquer A durable, protective resinous varnish capable of receiving a hard polish. Available with or without coloring pigments.

Lamination (Laminated wood): A type of plied wood in which the veneers (to be laminated) are placed so that the grain runs in the same direction. Like solid wood, laminated wood is strongest in the direction of grain. However, it surpasses solid wood's strength, as when utilized in laminated furniture.

Lathing The shaping of wood, metal, etc., by rotating on a lathe—a machine which turns the material horizontally against a cutting tool to achieve the desired form.

Marquetry A detailed, decorative design executed in a veneer. Contrasting materials, primarily wood, are cut to correspond to spaces in the veneer ground.

Neoprene An oil-resistant synthetic rubber.

Nickel plating The successful electroplating process as perfected during the 1860s. Nickel became a major choice for finishing metals during the early twentieth century. Due to its grayish tinge and tendency to tarnish, however, nickel was gradually replaced by the more attractive chromium plating during the mid 1920s. Chromium's extremely, shiny surface has a more retentive, purer white color.

Onyx Marble The present-day term for alabaster. A popular stone of ancient civilizations. Onyx marble is composed of strips of concentric zones of color (calcite or aragonite) on a creamy white field. (Not to be confused with onyx, the semiprecious stone.)

Open Planning A modern concept of space planning instigated by the American Frank Lloyd Wright at the turn of the twentieth century, in which traditional concepts of room and spatial arrangements gave way to large, flowing living areas which integrated compatible activities. Columns, plants, changes of floor and ceiling level, or furniture arrangements defined activity space instead of walls.

Organic Design When applied to furniture, a classification of design characterized by the harmonizing of parts and materials into one unified, consolidated form.

Plywood A layered veneered wood construction in which the direction of grain alternates. Therefore, unlike solid wood, plywood is equally strong in both directions.

Polyester fiber padding A popular batting for upholstered furniture, pillows, and quilts, made from highly crimped polyester fibers.

Quilted upholstery A multicomponent structure composed of surface fabrics and inner padding which are stitched together or fused with heat.

Resiliency A material's innate ability to return to its original state after being bent, stretched, or compressed.

Rosewood A valuable tropical cabinet wood found in India and South America; a fine-grained reddish brown wood with black streaks which is able to take a high polish.

Rubber-Weld Joint A joint constructed by bonding metal to rubber to wood. First employed in furniture construction by Charles and Ray Eames. (See Plywood Chair, Figure 34.)

Russian Constructivism A post-World War I art movement which originated in Moscow as a reaction against traditional fine art—sculpture in particular. As the name implies, Constructivists explored new concepts of structuring three-dimensional forms. Rejecting the traditional definition they stated that form also resulted from suggestion or outline of space and not from solid mass alone. New industrial materials, metal tubes, wires, and sheets of plastic or glass gave means for actualizing their ideas. In the area of furniture design, Vladimir Tatlin, Mart Stam, and Marcel Breuer produced examples of the "constructions in space" which embodied Constructivist thought. (See Wassily Chair, Figure 5.)

Saddle Leather A thick cut of cowhide for use in articles requiring a stable, durable covering without much flexibility. Saddle leather is utilized in shoes, harnesses, and saddles, as well as upholstery covers and supporting seat/back slings.

Sled Base A furniture support which glides easily across the floor. Instead of the weight of the furniture being concentrated on the traditional four legs, it is distributed along two runners which rest parallel along the floor.

Sling In furniture, a strap or band of flexible material, such as leather or fabric, which is only partly attached to a rigid frame, thus necessitating dimensional stability to resist distortion or bagging out of shape when used.

Stainless Steel An expensive alloy of steel produced by combining carbon, chromium, and nickel with steel, which results in a highly corrosion- and oxidation-resistant metal requiring no protective coating in use. *Mild Steel* is easier to work and cheaper than stainless steel, but must be coated with metal plate or enamel to prevent corrosion.

Stijl, de (The style) A Dutch design movement, started in 1917 by a group of artists and architects, which spread to become a major component of Rational design. Characterized by flat, smooth geometric planes and fundamental construction, de Stijl was founded on the theories of the Dutch architect Hendrik Berlage but drew additional influences from the earlier Cubist and Futurist movements. Frank Lloyd Wright was a direct influence on the most outstanding designer of de Stijl furniture, Gerrit Rietveld.

Strap Metal A thin strip of wrought iron.

Stretcher A horizontal bar which ties or braces the under framework of furniture.

Tandem A linear arrangement of seats supported on the same framework.

Template A rigid plate of metal, plastic, wood, etc., which serves as a pattern or guide. A frequently used mechanical design tool.

Three-Dimensionally Molded Describes a complex molded form in which curves occur in both lengthwise and crosswise directions. (See Plywood Chair, Fig. 34.)

Tooling The fitting of a factory or workshop with machines and equipment essential for its proper function.

Travertine A dense, banded limestone, light-colored and able to take a high polish. A frequent interior and exterior finishment.

Tubular Steel A hollow, cylinder-shaped pipe of steel, thin-walled in comparison to its overall diameter.

Tufting The drawing together of two surfaces (e.g., the front and back of an upholstery cushion) at regular points with stitches. Buttons are frequently added as a finishing over the resulting depressions.

Two-Dimensionally Molded Describes the bending of a flat piece of material in either its lengthwise or crosswise direction, not both. (See Aalto's Paimio Chair, Figure 23.)

Vulcanized Material which has been treated with heat and sulfur to improve its durability.

Welding The fusing of separate pieces of metal by first softening with heat and then uniting with pounding or a fusible binding material. In 1916 the oxyacetylene process (blowtorch) was perfected for constructing World War I airplanes. This process enabled the butt welding of tubes and bars, as used in furniture of the following decade.

Welting In furniture, a piping, with or without cording, stitched into the seams of a cushion which increases the durability of the seam.

Wrought Iron Iron which is fashioned by means of pounding out with hammers. In contrast to cast iron, which is formed by pouring molten iron into a mold, wrought iron is highly malleable and stronger.

Bibliography

Aalto, Elissa: Personal interview conducted by Charles Gandy, Helsinki, Finland, November 1978.

Abercrombie, Stanley: "Marcel Breuer: A Retrospective," *Contract Interiors*, vol. 136, no. 2 (September 1977), pp. 98–109.

Alison, Filippo: *Charles Rennie Mackintosh as a Designer of Chairs*, Woodbury, New York, Barrons, 1977.

Alvar Aalto, 1898–1976, Helsinki, The Museum of Finnish Architecture, Yhteiskirjapaino, Printers, 1978.

Anderson, John: "Designs for Living," *Playboy*, vol. 8 (July 1961), pp. 46–92, 108–110.

Architecture and Furniture, New York, The Museum of Modern Art, 1938.

Armluster, William: "Steel Furniture," *Progressive Architecture*, vol. 42 (September 1961), pp. 198–203.

"As the Bough Is Bent," *Interiors*, vol. 106, no. 101 (May 1947), pp. 126–128.

Baker, Geoffrey: "Organic Design," *Magazine of Art*, vol. 34, no. 9, (November 1941) pp. 482–483, 492–493.

Banham, Reyner: *Theory and Design in the First Machine Age*, London, The Architectural Press, 1960.

Battersby, Martin: *The History of Furniture*, New York, William Morrow & Company, Inc., 1976.

Bauhaus, Stuttgart, Institut für Auslandbeziehungen, 1975.

Bayer, Herbert, Walter Gropius, and Andise Gropius (eds.): *Bauhaus, 1919–1928*, New York, The Museum of Modern Art, 1975.

Benton, Tim, Charlotte Benton, and Denis Sharp: *Form and Function: A Source Book for the History of Architecture and Design 1890–1939*, London, Crosby Lockwood Staples in assn. with the Open University Press, 1975.

Besset, Maurice: *Who Was Le Corbusier?* translated from the French by Robin Kembell, Geneva, Skira; distributed in the United States by The World Publishing Company, Cleveland, 1968.

"Best of New Furniture," *Interiors*, vol. 108 (October 1948), pp. 92–101.

Blair, Alan (translator): *Alvar Aalto*, Zurich: Verlag für Architektur, 1963.

Blake, Peter: *Marcel Breuer: Architect and Designer*, New York, Architectural Record Book, in collaboration with The Museum of Modern Art, 1949.

———: "Modern Antiques: Twentieth Century Landmarks," *Architectural Forum*, vol. 136 (May 1967), pp. 80–81.

———*The Master Builders*, New York, Alfred A. Knopf, Inc., 1960.

Breuer, Marcel: *Sun and Shadow*, ed. Peter Blake; London, Longmans, Green and Company, 1956.

Camp, Holly: "The Serious Business of Show and Tell," *Signature*, Diners Club Inc., 1974.

Caplan, Ralph: *Connections: The Work of Charles and Ray Eames*, Los Angeles, Fredrick S. Wright Art Gallery, University of California, 1976.

———: *The Design of Herman Miller: Pioneered by Eames, Girard, Nelson, Propst, Rohe*, New York, Whitney Library of Design, 1976.

Carter, Peter: "Eero Saarinen 1910–1961," *Architectural Design*, vol. 31 (December 1961), p. 537.

———: *Mies van der Rohe at Work*, New York, Praeger, 1974.

"Charles Eames, Creator in Plywood," *Interiors*, vol. 105, no. 12, (December 1946) pp. 53–59.

Conroy, Sarah Booth: "Charles Eames, Innovator in Modern U.S. Design, Dies," *The Washington Post*, August 24, 1978, p. 8 col. 1.

———: "The Mystery of the Designing Lovers," *International Herald Tribune*, March 17, 1977, p. 5, cols. 3–8.

Cresti, Carlo: *Alvar Aalto*: Gestafler unserer Zeit, Lucerne, Switzerland, Kunstkreis Luzem, 1975.

Daniel, Greta: "Thonet Furniture," general introductory caption for the New York Museum of Modern Art's exhibition, August 12 through October 4, 1953.

Darrach, Betsy: "Wegner," *Interiors*, vol. 118 (February 1959), pp. 82–85.

Das Haus Thonet, Frankenberg, Germany, Gebrüder Thonet.

De Fusco, Renato: *Le Corbusier, Designer: Furniture, 1929*, Milan, Gruppo Editoriale Electa, SpA, 1976.

Delong, James: "Mies . . . His Eloquent Legacy: Purity of Structure," *House Beautiful* (November 1969), pp. 132–133.

Di Puelo, Maurizio, Marcello Fagilol, and Maria Luisa Madonna: *Le Corbusier, Charlotte Perriand, Pierre Jeanneret: "La Machine à s'asseoir,"* Rome, De Luca Editore, 1976.

Drexler, Arthur: *Charles Eames: Furniture from the Design Collection*, New York, The Museum of Modern Art, 1973.

———: *Ludwig Mies van der Rohe*, New York, George Braziller, Inc., 1960.

Dunhill, Priscilla: "Gerry Griffith: Master Craftsman in Stainless Steel," *Interiors*. vol. 124 (November 1964), pp. 74–75.

Dyer, Walter A., and Esther Stevens Fraser: *The Rocking Chair: An American Institution*, New York, The Century Co., 1978.

Eames, Ray: Personal communications to Gandy Zimmermann-Stidham regarding life and work of Charles Eames, Fall 1979.

Eckstein, Hans: *Der Stuhl: Funktion, Konstruktion, Form von d. Antike bis zur Gegenwart*, Munich, Keyserische Verlagsbuchhandlung GmbH, 1977.

"Eero Saarinen: 1910–1961," *Interiors*, vol 121 (November 1961), pp. 128–131.

Filler, Martin: "Bending with the Times," *Progressive Architecture*, vol. 59, no. 2 (February 1978), pp. 74–77.

Finnish Society of Crafts and Design: "Aalto: Interior Architecture, Furniture and Furnishings," *Progressive Architecture*. vol. 58 (April 1977).

Form From Process: The Thonet Chair, exhibition catalog, Carpenter Center for the Visual Arts, Cambridge, Mass., Harvard University, 1967.

Frey, Gilbert: *The Modern Chair: 1850 to Today,* Teufen, Switzerland, Arthur Niggli, Ltd., 1970.

"From the Classes to the Masses," *Progressive Architecture,* vol. 51 (June 1970), pp. 150–155.

Gardiner, Stephen: *Le Corbusier,* London, Fontana Collins, 1974.

Giedion, Sigfried: "Alvar Aalto," *Architectural Review,* vol. 107 (January 1950), p. 84.

————: *Mechanization Takes Command: A Contribution to an Anonymous History,* New York, W. W. Norton & Company, Inc., 1969 (originally published by Oxford University Press, 1948).

————: *Space, Time and Architecture: The Growth of a New Tradition,* 5th ed., Cambridge, Mass., Harvard University Press, 1967.

Glaeser, Ludwig: *Ludwig Mies van der Rohe: Furniture and Furniture Drawings from the Design Collection and the Mies van der Rohe Archive,* New York, The Museum of Modern Art, 1977.

Glaog, John: *Victorian Comfort: A Social History of Design from 1830–1900,* London, David & Charles Ltd., 1973.

Goldstone, Harmon Hendricks: "Alvar Aalto," *Magazine of Art,* vol. 32, no. 4 (April 1939), pp. 208–221.

Gough, Marion: "Hans J. Wegner: Poet of Practicality," *House Beautiful,* vol. 101 (July 1959), pp. 65–71, 114.

Gutheim, Frederick: *Alvar Aalto,* New York, George Braziller, Inc., 1960.

Haskell, Douglas: "Eero Saarinen 1910–1961," *Architectural Forum,* vol. 115 (October 1961), pp. 96–97.

Hatje, Gerd, and Karl Kaspar (eds.), *New Furniture,* vol. 7, Stuttgart, Verlag Gerd Hatje, 1964.

———— and ———— (eds.), *New Furniture,* vol. 8, Stuttgart, Verlag Gerd Hatje, 1966.

Heyer, Paul: *Architects on Architecture,* New York, Walker & Company, 1966.

"Hi Mister Eames!" *Arbitare,* vol. 86 (June–July 1970), pp. 42–45.

Honour, Hugh: *Cabinet Makers and Furniture Designers,* London, Hamlyn Publishing Group Ltd., 1972.

Hornung, Clarence P.: *Treasury of American Design,* New York, Harry N. Abrams, Inc., 1972.

Hughes, Robert: "Doing Their Own Thing," *Time,* vol. 113, no. 2 (January 8, 1979), pp. 32–39.

"An Interview with Hans J. Wegner." *Interior Design,* vol. 45 (June 1974), pp. 58 and 68.

Jencks, Charles: *Le Corbusier and the Tragic View of Architecture,* Cambridge, Mass., Harvard University Press, 1973.

Johnson, Philip C.: *Machine Art: March 6 to April 30, 1934,* New York, The Museum of Modern Art, 1934.

————: *Mies van der Rohe,* New York, The Museum of Modern Art, 1947.

Jones, Cranston: *Marcel Breuer: Buildings & Projects, 1921–1961,* London, Thames and Hudson, 1962.

Joyce, Ernest: *The Encyclopedia of Furniture Making,* New York, Drake Publishing Inc. 1970.

Kane, Patricia E.: *300 Years of American Seating,* Boston, Little, Brown, and Company, 1976.

Kaufmann, Edgar, Jr.: *Prize Designs for Modern Furniture from the International Competition for Low-Cost Furniture Design,* New York, The Museum of Modern Art, 1950.

"Le Corbu," *Architectural Forum,* vol. 123 (October 1965).

"Le Corbusier, Pioneering Architect, Is Dead," *New York Times,* Aug. 28, 1965, p. 1., col. 2.

Lessing, Lawrence: "The Diversity of Eero Saarinen," *Architectural Forum,* vol. 113 (July 1960), pp. 94–103.

Logie, Gordon: *Furniture From Machines,* London, George Allen & Unwin Ltd., 1974.

McQuade, Walter: "Eero Saarinen: A Complete Architect," *Architectural Forum,* vol. 116 (April 1962), pp. 102–119.

Madsen, Stephan Tschudi: *Sources of Art Nouveau,* New York, George Wittenborn, Inc., 1955.

Mang, Karl: *Geschichte des Modernen Möbels,* Stuttgart, Gerd Hatje, 1978.

————, and Eva Mang: *Bentwood Furniture: The Work of Michael Thonet,* exhibition catalog, Great Britain, Bethnal Green Museum, 1968.

Masheck, Joseph: "Embalmed Objects: Design at the Modern," *Art Forum,* vol. 13 (February 1975), pp. 49–54.

Meadmore, Clement: *The Modern Chair: Classics in Production,* London, Studio Vista, 1974.

"Nelson, Eames, Girad, Propst: The Design Process at Herman Miller," *Design Quarterly 98–99,* Minneapolis, Walker Art Center, 1975.

Nelson, George: "Modern Furniture," *Interiors,* vol. 108, no. 12 (July 1949), pp. 77–117.

"New Furniture by Marcel Breuer," *Interiors,* vol. 106, no. 7 (February 1947), pp. 90–94.

Nielsen, Johan Møller: *Wegner: en dansk møbelkunster,* Copenhagen, Gyldendal, 1965.

Papachristou, Tician: *Marcel Breuer: New Buildings and Projects,* New York, Frederick A. Praeger, Inc., 1970.

Papi, Lorenzo: *Ludwig Mies van der Rohe,* Florence, G. C. Sansoni, 1975.

Pearson, Paul David: *Alvar Aalto and the International Style,* New York, Whitney Library of Design, 1978.

Pevsner, Nikolaus: *Pioneers of Modern Design: From William Morris to Walter Gropius,* Middlesex, England, Penguin Books, 1960 (originally published as *Pioneers of the Modern Movement,* London, Faber & Faber, Ltd., 1936).

Rea, Richard D.: "Classic Bentwood Chair," *Woodworking & Furniture Digest,* March 1976.

Saarinen, Aline B.: *Eero Saarinen on his Work,* New Haven, Conn., Yale University Press, 1966 (revised 1968).

"Saarinen Places Furniture on a Pedestal," *Architectural Record,* vol. 122 (July 1957), p. 284.

Schildt, Göran: Personal communication to Gandy/Zimmermann-Stidham regarding life and work of Alvar Aalto, Ekenäs, Finland, Dec. 11, 1978.

Schulz, Karin: *Charles Eames,* Basel, Switzerland, Herman Miller AG, 1976.

Sekler, Eduard F.: "Mackintosh in Vienna," from *The Anti-Rationalists* by Nikolaus Pevsner & J. M. Richards, Toronto, University of Toronto Press, 1973.

Serenyi, Peter: *Le Corbusier in Perspective,* Englewood Cliffs, N.J., Prentice-Hall, Inc., 1975.

"Shock Proof Furniture," *Architectural Forum,* vol 84, no. 4 (April 1946), pp. 84–85.

Smithson, A. & P.: "Eames Celebration," *Architectural Design,* vol. 36 (September 1966), entire issue.

Temko, Allan: *Eero Saarinen,* New York, George Braziller, 1962.

"Thonet 1830–1953," exhibition catalog, New York, The Museum of Modern Art.

The Thonet Story, York, Pennsylvania, Thonet Industries.

Wegner, Hans J.: Personal interview conducted by Gandy and Zimmermann-Stidham, Copenhagen, November 1978.

"Wegner Retrospective: Exhibition at Jensen's," *Interiors,* vol. 124 (May 1965), pp. 14–16.

Whitman, Alden: "Mies van der Rohe Dies at 83; Leader of Modern Architecture," *New York Times,* Aug. 9, 1969, p. 1., col. 2.

Wingler, Hans M.: *Das Bauhaus,* Bramsche: Verlag Gebr. Rasch & Co., 1962 (revised 1975).

Wrede, Stuart: "An Archeology of Aalto," *Progressive Architecture,* vol. 58 (April 1977), pp. 57–67.

Yee, Roger: "Sloughing Towards Barcelona," *Progressive Architecture,* vol. 106, no. 2 (February 1975), pp. 78–85.

Index

Page numbers in **boldface** refer to illustrations.

Drawing Credits

Figs. 1–4: Gebrüder Thonet
Figs. 5–9, 11–14, 16, 17, 23, 25–29, 34–36
  37c, 39-42: Keri Z. Allen
Figs. 10, 30–33: The Office of Hans J. Wegner
Figs. 37 *a, b:* The Office of Charles and Ray Eames
Figs. 18–22: Cassina, S.p.A.

Photo Credits

Figs. 1–3: Gebrüder Thonet
Fig. 4: Thonet Industries
Figs. 5–8: Knoll International, Inc.
Fig. 9: International Contract Furnishings, Inc.
Figs. 10–14: Knoll International, Inc.
Figs. 15–17: Retoria/Y. Futagawa
Fig. 18: Atelier International, Ltd.
Figs. 19, 20: Cassina, S.p.A.
Figs. 21, 22: Atelier International, Inc.
Fig. 23: International Contract Furnishings, Inc.
Figs. 24–29: Artek
Fig. 30: Knoll International, Inc.
Figs. 31–33: Johannes Hansen
Figs. 34–37: The Office of Charles and Ray Eames
Figs. 38–42: Knoll International, Inc.

About the Authors

Charles D. Gandy, A.S.I.D., is president of C. Gandy & Associates, a multidisciplined design firm based in Atlanta, Georgia. He is also vice president of the Georgia chapter of the American Society of Interior Designers, and has taught on the faculty of the American College for the Applied Arts in Atlanta, Georgia. He has been program director for The American Institute of Interior Design in Switzerland, a division of The American College of Lucerne. He has for some years successfully designed both residential and commercial interiors.

Susan Zimmermann-Stidham taught interior design and furniture history for several years at The American Institute of Interior Design, a division of The American College of Lucerne. When at the University of Georgia, from which she has a degree in Interior Design, she was a representative to the Georgia chapter of A.I.D. (today the A.S.I.D.). She resides today in Lucerne, Switzerland, where she continues research for forthcoming references on furniture history.